AMERICAN INSTITUTE OF CERTIFIED PUBLIC ACCOUNTANTS

A CPA's Guide to
High-Risk Investment Strategies:

Derivatives, Options, Straddles, and Other Hedges

D.L. Smith, MBA, CPA, JD

Notice to Readers

A CPA's Guide to High-Risk Investment Strategies: Derivatives, Options, Straddles, and Other Hedges does not represent an official position of the American Institute of Certified Public Accountants, and it is distributed with the understanding that the author and publisher are not rendering legal, accounting, or other professional services in this publication. If legal advice or other expert assistance is required, the services of a competent professional should be sought.

ISBN 0–87051–228–5

In the early 1980s, many new financial instruments were created to serve financial goals of corporations who sought to manage risk associated with fluctuations in interest and currency markets. These innovative techniques are often complex, full of contingencies and restrictions. They are often misunderstood (if understood at all). As a result—as anyone reading a newspaper in the last few years knows—a number of problems have arisen.

This book takes on the broad mission of defining these financial instruments by explaining how they are created, what they are designed to accomplish, and what are their tax consequences. Although press reports have tended to concentrate on the disastrous effects of the misuse of derivatives, and by doing so, vilify these financial instruments, this book attempts to educate the reader by replacing the hysteria with understanding.

We are grateful to the author of this book, D.L. Smith, for his commitment to such a daunting project. Mr. Smith, a CPA and attorney, is also the author of the popular AICPA course, *Investment Strategies in the 90s*. He is a specialist in the areas of tax and financial planning.

We thank Richard Shapiro, Esq., Tax Partner in the Financial Services Industry Practice of Ernst & Young, LLP, for his comprehensive technical review of the course on which this book is based.

Mary Schantz
Vice President, Product Development

TABLE OF CONTENTS

CHAPTER 3 — FUTURES, FORWARDS, AND OTHER DERIVATIVE PRODUCTS   33

CHAPTER 4 — INTEREST RATE SWAPS   43

CHAPTER 1

INTRODUCTION

OBJECTIVE

After completing this chapter you will understand:

- The building blocks used to create sophisticated financial products.
- The basic economic and financial aspects of the four basic financial products.
- The basic tax principles relating to these products.

INTRODUCTION

A host of new financial instruments were developed during the early eighties. Almost all of these instruments were designed to serve financial goals related to managing risk due to fluctuations in interest and currency markets. Corporations employing innovative financing techniques have issued financial instruments containing various restrictions, rights, and contingencies consistent with the credit markets in which they employ capital, or borrow from. As corporations have ventured into many of the new international marketplaces, the credit markets, associated with doing business in these international markets, also need to be managed.

Generally, corporations have turned to financial institutions for help. Looking to provide the best bang for the buck and to avoid many of the transaction costs associated with hedging these risks, many of these financial institutions have created very complex instruments to protect the corporation from many risks they could suffer. What has developed is an instrument that allows a corporation to manage a combination of risks through the issuance of a single instrument.

Analyzing these new financial instruments requires an understanding of the underlying risks that these instruments are trying to protect against. Critical is an analysis of possible cash flows investors can expect to pay or receive. Also critical is an understanding of how and why the instrument was created and what tax advantage, if any, the seller or purchaser intends to receive.

Some financial instruments contain features that would justify characterizing debt instruments as equity interests and vice versa. Many of these financial instruments do not fit easily into any of the categories formulated by the tax laws, and the treatment of some still remains unclear. Given the complexities of the problems involved, the IRS, Treasury, and Congress have not been able to respond fully to how they intend to tax some of these financial instruments, and therefore the tax consequences attaching to transactions involving these instruments are still speculative.

Trying to fit any of these new financial instruments into a single mold is generally a mistake and will serve only to confuse. However, these new financial instruments are generally a combination of the more basic financial instruments that investors are used to seeing. Therefore, knowledge of the basic types of standard contracts offered is essential.

The chapters that follow will attempt to break down some of the more sophisticated financial instruments into their component parts, permitting readers to understand the financial and tax consequences of the financial instruments discussed.

BASIC FINANCIAL INSTRUMENTS

Generally, derivative financial products contain one or more financial instruments which can be classified into four basic categories:

- Debt (principal and interest);
- Spot or cash physical positions (which include commodities and equity positions);
- Futures, forwards and swaps; and
- Options.

DEBT

Debt is created when a person borrows or lends property. Property could be money, but could also be other property. For instance, one could borrow shares of stock in a corporation (i.e., AT&T stock), a foreign currency (i.e., French francs), or a commodity (i.e., bushels of corn). Principal is the money or other property borrowed. Interest is the charge for the use of the borrowed money or property. Depending on the property borrowed, interest will reflect:

1. The cost of funds or time value of money at the time of the borrowing;

2. The risk that the borrower will not repay the borrowed property;

3. Plus any income that the property would have earned during the borrowed period;

4. Less any costs that the lender avoids while the property is borrowed (e.g., insurance and storage costs).

When cash is borrowed interest simply represents the cost of funds plus the risk of non-repayment. Most derivative products are created to hedge the risk associated with changes in interest rates. As corporations commit themselves to borrowing to finance their business operations, changes in the interest rate are a continuing concern. The longer the commitment the greater the concern. Consider two treasury obligations, both yielding 8%: the 3-year treasury note and the 20-year treasury bond. A 2% increase in interest rates will result in a 17% decrease in the principal of the 20-year treasury bond, while a 2% increase in interest rates will result in between a 3–4% change in the principal value of the note.

Most debt associated with derivative products have terms different from the typical lending transaction. In the typical lending transaction, a fixed sum is lent for a fixed period of time in return for a fixed rate of interest. Some derivative financial instruments call for no interest to be paid until the maturity date (zero coupon obligations); others "strip-out" only the interest for a specific time period, while others index the interest rate wholly or partially to the price of the underlying property. However, all debt obligations, upon careful analysis, can be reduced to three basic components: interest, principal, and one or more imbedded financial instruments — usually an option, forward or future.

SPOT OR CASH PHYSICAL POSITIONS

The category includes the cash market for commodities and other property, other than money. The spot market includes equity, physical commodities and foreign currency.

Equities traditionally represent an ownership interest in a company without the expectation of repayment of the amount invested. Debt is distinguished in that the investment is expected to be repaid. When considering derivative products, debt is generally distinguished from equity based on whether the investor is guaranteed repayment of the amount invested. This is true regardless of the label attached to the instrument.

Along with the debt versus distinction comes the determination of whether the payout constitutes interest and whether the payout will generate ordinary income, or capital gain or loss.

Physical commodities generally fall into two categories: natural resources and precious metals like gold, silver and oil, and agricultural products like cattle, corn, hogs and wheat.

Foreign currency is generally a delivery of or in a currency other than the currency that the investor transacts business in. For U.S. investors, it will be other than the U.S. dollar.

The spot or cash price for a commodity or other property is the price that a willing buyer and seller would agree to immediately exchange, for cash, the commodity or other property, that is, the current market price quoted for the commodity or other property. The spot market is not interest sensitive, in that it does not consider the future value of the commodity or other property. Where the delivery period is not immediate, it is ignored by the market and the pricing considers only today's value.

FUTURES, FORWARDS AND SWAPS

Futures and forwards are contracts to buy or sell a commodity at some specified date in the future for a price agreed upon today.

The futures contract is a standardized contract, in that the quantity, time, and place of delivery are standardized. In the U.S., a futures contract must be traded on a futures exchange regulated by the Commodity Futures Trading Commission (CFTC).[1]

The terms of forward contracts are not standardized and are not regulated by an exchange. Forward contracts are private agreements made by means of informal trading networks and markets. For instance, a forward contract could require delivery of a specified quantity and grade of a commodity on a particular date without an established price, although the mechanism for determining the price will be specified in the contract. Because forward contracts are privately negotiated, the parties will look to each other for performance. Additionally, the contracts are generally not assignable or capable of being closed out by offset without the agreement of both parties. Therefore, another main difference between a future and a forward contract is that a forward contract contemplates delivery of the underlying commodity.

To further complicate matters, certain forwards are cash settled, meaning they do not require delivery.

Both the future and forward require the parties to transact the sale/purchase at the specified terms on the specified date. For example, X agrees to sell Y 60 bushels of wheat in six months for 50 cents a bushel. The contractual obligations of both parties are set. When the contract matures, both parties are obligated to perform their side of the bargain. The markets in which these contracts trade will determine the future spot price of the commodity. Forward contracts are priced by adding interest and carrying charges to the spot price.

There are three ways to settle a futures or a forward contract:

1. Physical delivery of the underlying commodity;

2. Cash-settlement; or

3. Another offsetting position or forward contract.

Both futures and forwards can be disposed before maturity. A futures contract can be closed out on an exchange by buying an offsetting position. Forward contracts can also be settled before maturity with the loser ("the party with the leg that has declined in value") negotiating with the winner to pay the winner the difference between the value of the contract on the date it was opened and the value on the date it is closed.

A swap is an executory contract which is based on a notional (made-up) principal amount. No exchange of principal amounts is contemplated and the notional principal amount is used only as a determinant of the payments to be made under the contract. Economically, swaps mimic futures and forwards. In fact, swaps are priced as a series of forward contracts with staggered maturity dates. The prices of the forward contracts are averaged and the single, averaged price becomes the strike price at each settlement date.

Swaps can be extinguished by cash settlement or assignment. In a cash settlement, the party that is the net loser on the swap contract at the date of extinguishment pays the net winner the present value of the remaining obligation of the swap. If the swap is assigned, the assignee (party that wants to get out of the swap) assigns the position to the assignor (the party that agrees to take over the swap position), a payment is made to the above-water party equal to the present value of the remaining obligation of the swap. A party to a swap can also extinguish market risk by entering into an offsetting position. Both the original swap and the offsetting swap will remain outstanding, however the market risk is eliminated.

OPTIONS

Options are bilateral executory contracts conveying rights or obligations (but not both) to buy or sell the underlying property which is the object of the contract. An option contract entitles the holder (purchaser of the contract) for the payment of a premium (the cost of the contract) to exercise his rights under the contract (i.e., purchase the underlying property) from the writer (the seller of the contract) at the strike price (negotiated cost of property) at any time before or on the exercise date.

The difference between an option and a spot contract is that the seller's right to demand a price for the contract is inseparable from the actual delivery of the underlying property. That is, even where the price for the underlying property is determined some time in the future, delivery is contemplated by the terms of the contract.

A right to purchase the underlying property is a "call" option, whereas the right to sell the property is a "put" option. A holder or purchaser of an option is said to be long and the writer or seller is said to be short the option.

The holder of a call option will exercise his option only if the market price of the underlying property, on the exercise date, is more than the strike price of the option. Similarly, the holder of a put option would exercise his option only if the market price of the underlying property, on the exercise date, is less than the strike price of the option. If the strike price is not attractive, the holder is not obligated to purchase or sell the underlying property. Therefore, an option can be viewed as one-half of a futures or forward contract. Where a future or forward contract obligates the holder or writer to both the increase and decrease in the price of the underlying property, an option contract allows (for the contract premium) the writer to profit and the holder to walk away if the purchase is uneconomical.

For example, assume that X believes the price of commodity A is likely to increase over the next six months. X can enter into a forward or futures contract for the purchase of commodity X at $50/unit which sets the price at $50/unit regardless of the actual price at the time X takes delivery of commodity A. Thus, if X is correct and the price of commodity A rises to $60/unit, X has a winning position with regard to commodity A. However, X is obligated to buy commodity A at $50/unit, even if the price of commodity A decreases to $40/unit. The purchase of an option avoids the downside risk. If X purchases an option to purchase commodity A at $50/unit, and the price falls below $50/unit, X can allow the option to lapse unexercised and buy the commodity on the open market. Therefore, when an investor purchases an option, if the prices fall, the investor's loss is limited to the premium (price) paid for the option.

There are two types of option contracts, American and European. An American contract entitles the holder to purchase the underlying property at any time up to the exercise date. A European option contract entitles the holder to purchase the underlying property only on the exercise date.

Options on futures contracts give the holder the right to purchase or sell futures contracts in a given commodity. A long call option to acquire futures settles in a long futures contract, a short call in a short futures contract. A long put settles in a short futures contract, a short put in a long futures contract.

Options on futures contracts are a way of isolating or separating the movement in the price of the commodity, i.e., to separate the risk of falling prices from the benefit of rising prices. For example, a long call and a short put are equivalent to a long futures contract. Conversely, a short call and a long put are equal to a short futures contract.

ANALYSIS

To demonstrate the analysis of a derivative financial product consider the following complex derivative offered by the credit facility of a major international auto manufacturer (T). T in the beginning of 1994 issued an index or structured note. The interest payment was based on the following formula:

Principal * [16.5% − (2 * 3yr DKR Swap)], Min 0.

That is, the interest coupon was based on a rate of 16.5% less two times the three year Danish kroner swap rate, but in no event could the investor be required to refund principal.

Using the analysis described above, because the principal is guaranteed the instrument would be classified as debt. The guarantee is in the form of a Cap (described above as Min 0). Caps will be discussed in greater detail in Chapter 4. Briefly, a Cap is an interest rate agreement whereby one of the counterparties agrees to limit the floating rate of interest to a set rate. In the above case, the rate is limited to the rate at which the interest payment would go below zero. Further, since the rate of interest will decrease as interest rates increase, this derivative debt instrument contains an inverse floater. An inverse floater can best be described as being long a fixed rate future and short a floating rate future. Additionally, the inverse floating rate is determined by the three year Danish kroner swap rate. This rate will usually be determined by dealer quotes. Given the three year rate, the instrument will have a constant maturity with regard to the inverse interest rate chosen. The structured note could have used a floating maturity, i.e., something tied to short-term treasury obligations.

To continue, since the rate decreases at twice the rate of the three year Danish kroner, the investor has purchased a leveraged instrument. Lastly, the investor will have to bear the currency risk of the Danish kroner (assuming a non-Danish investor).

To re-cap: the above instrument represents a straight debt obligation with a constant maturity three years, with four different financial instruments imbedded therein—an inverse floater (long fixed rate short floating rate interest rate future) plus a leveraged Danish currency forward and a long Cap.

It should be noted that the above structured note, although not uncommon, is a very sophisticated derivative financial instrument. It is analyzed to demonstrate the complexity of these instruments, along with demonstrating that dividing the instrument into its component parts is the only way to truly analyze these instruments. Remember, by creating such an instrument T was trying to hedge each of the above identified risks. Combining all the risks in one instrument makes it easier for T to control these risks. It also makes it a nightmare for investors.

One other point, if you were not able to identify all the financial instruments imbedded within the above debt instrument, do not be discouraged. Each of these financial instruments will be developed over the chapters to follow.

ORIGINAL ISSUE DISCOUNT

As we have described above, there are two components to a debt instrument: principal (the amount that is borrowed) and interest (the amount that is charged for borrowing the principal). The general purpose of original issue discount (OID) is to properly categorize interest as interest and principal as principal. The OID rules require that a market rate of interest is economically accrued and included in income in the appropriate period by the taxpayer.[2]

For example, a two-year bond with a stated redemption price of $1,000 is issued for $857. The bond does not pay interest. The discount of $143 ($1,000 – $857) is equal to the present value of receiving a payment of 8% annually. The $143 is OID.

The primary purpose of the OID rules is to ensure that interest is recognized as it economically accrues. The OID rules provide that this accrual is to be accounted for daily, i.e., the ratable daily portion that has accrued during the period is included, whereas stated interest is included in the taxpayer's income under his regular method of accounting.[3] For example, if the taxpayer is on the cash method, he would include interest in income as it is received for tax purposes.

To determine whether a debt instrument calls for an adequate stated interest (whether the debt instrument provides for a market rate of interest), it is necessary to test the stated interest rate against the applicable federal rate (AFR).[4]

The AFR is the rate determined by the Secretary of the Treasury, monthly, based on the average market yield on outstanding market obligations of the U.S. with similar maturities. The taxpayer can choose from the current or previous two months' rates. This two-month lookback allows taxpayers to have a degree of certainty regarding the applicable rate of interest.[5]

Debt instruments with a term of not more than three years use the short-term published rate. Debt instruments with a term of more than three years but not more than nine years use the mid-term published rate, and debt instruments with a term of more than nine years use the long-term published rate.[6]

Where the debt is issued for cash the calculation is straightforward; however, difficulties are presented when the debt is issued for non-publicly traded ("hard to value") property or where the parties are not dealing at arm's length.

To determine whether there is OID in an instrument, the stated redemption price at maturity is compared to the issue price and the qualified stated interest. The stated redemption price at maturity is defined as the sum of all payments provided by the debt instrument other than qualified stated interest payments.[7] Qualified stated interest is defined as stated interest that is unconditionally payable (or will be constructively received) in cash or other property at least annually at a single fixed rate.[8] The single fixed rate must take into account the interval between payments.[9]

If the debt instrument is subject to one or more contingencies, the contingencies must be analyzed. If the contingency is other than remote, the issuer must provide a projected payment schedule for the debt instrument and interest will accrue according to the projected payment schedule.[10] The tax treatment of contingent debt instruments will be considered in detail in Chapter 5.

Some debt instruments provide for interest holidays or other interest shortfalls. If this is the case, the stated redemption price at maturity is deemed to be the instrument's issue price plus the greater of the forgone interest or the excess of the stated principal amount over the issue price.

In some cases OID may be de minimis (less than 1/4 of one-percent of the stated redemption price at maturity multiplied by the number of years to maturity).[11] De minimis OID is generally included in income in the same proportion as the principal payments.[12]

The amount of OID is computed using the constant yield method.[13] Computationally, the following steps are required:

1. Determine the instrument's yield to maturity;[14]

2. Determine the accrual period;[15]

3. Determine the OID allocable to accrual period;[16]

4. If the accrual period spans two taxable years, allocate the daily portion of the OID attributable to the accrual period.

SUMMARY

We have described the four basic types of financial instruments which can be used to construct more sophisticated financial instruments: debt; spot and physical positions (which include commodities and equity positions); futures, forwards and swaps; and options. Each of the four types of financial instruments can be used to hedge different underlying risks and accomplish different financial goals and create many of the complex financial instruments offered by financial institutions and other corporations. Breaking down these complex instruments into their basic components will help investors analyze these new financial instruments, and develop an understanding of the underlying risks, cash flows and how and why the instrument was created. The upcoming chapters will develop the economic and tax principles underlying these basic financial instruments.

ENDNOTES

[1] See Commodity Exchange Act Section 4(a), 7 USC Section 6(a); USCS Section 6(a) (1982).

[2] IRC Section 1272.

[3] Reg. Sec. 1.1272-1(a).

[4] IRC Section 1274.

[5] IRC Section 1274(d)(1)(B).

[6] IRC Section 1274(d).

[7] Reg. Sec. 1.1273-1(b).

[8] Reg. Sec. 1.1273-1(c).

[9] Reg. Sec. 1.1273-1(c)(1)(iii).

[10] Prop. Reg. Sec. 1.1275-4(b)(4).

[11] IRC Section 1273(a)(3).

[12] Reg. Sec. 1.1273-1(d)(5)(i).

[13] Reg. Sec. 1.1273-1(b)(1).

[14] Reg. Sec. 1.1273-1(b)(1)(i).

[15] Reg. Sec. 1.1273-1(b)(1)(ii).

[16] Reg. Sec. 1.1273-1(b)(1)(iii).

CHAPTER 2

OPTIONS

OBJECTIVE

After completing this chapter you will understand:

- The basic economic and financial effects of options.

- How options are used to control risk.

- The tax effects of the options, rights and warrants.

INTRODUCTION

An option is a security whose value is linked to the underlying asset, and in that regard, an option is a derivative security. As financial institutions and corporations struggle with interest rate risks and the risks associated with obtaining the commodities they need to manufacture the products they produce, options offer downside protection at the same time ensuring that the necessary commodities will be available at the specified price.

For purposes of explaining the principles of an option, we will review the specifics of an equity option. The price of the option fluctuates as the price of the underlying stock rises and falls. Splits and stock dividends in the underlying stock will also affect the terms of the option, although cash dividends do not. Option holders do not receive cash dividends.

DEFINITION

An option is a contract under the terms of which:

1. The grantor — the writer of the option,

2. In exchange for consideration — the premium,

3. Undertakes an obligation to purchase from or sell to the other party to the contract — the holder,

4. A specific item or specific items of property at an agreed on price — the exercise or striking price.

The obligation will lapse if the holder does not exercise his right on or before a specified date, the expiration date. Where the option grants to the holder the right to purchase the property at the exercise price, it is usually referred to as a "call" option; where the grantor is obligated to purchase the property from the holder at the exercise price, the option is usually referred to as a "put" option.

A call option is said to be "in-the-money" if the stock price is above the strike price of the option, and "out-of-the-money" if the stock is selling below the strike price. The converse is true for put options. For example, DBL stock is trading at $112. The DBL March 110 call option is outofthemoney, just like the DBL June 110 call and the DBL March 120 call. However, the DBL March 100 call is in-the-money.

OPTION EXCHANGES

The listed option exchanges have standardized the terms of options contracts. In the listed option market, the issuer of all options is the exchange. Options on stock and securities are traded on the exchanges regulated by the SEC. Options on commodities and futures contracts are traded on exchanges regulated by the CFTC. Where futures trading in stock indexes is permitted, options on such indexes are traded on CFTC regulated exchanges. Options on other stock indexes are traded on SEC regulated exchanges. The following chapters describe the standardized option terms of the Option Clearing Corporation (OCC) and the mechanics of stock option transactions. They are identical to those relating to listed options on other types of property. It is important to understand the basics of how the Exchanges function to successfully implement any derivative investment strategy.

Standardized Contracts

1. Expiration Dates

   Listed options expire not more than nine months from the date granted; they expire quarterly on the Saturday following the third Friday of the expiration month. Quarterly schedules have one of three fixed cycles:

   a. The January, April, July, October cycle,
   b. The February, May, August, November cycle, or
   c. The March, June, September, December cycle.

   The above cycles permit an option grantor (sometimes referred to as the "writer") to select the desired expiration date. Option trades are settled on the next business day. Longer-term options called LEAPS (Long-term Equity Anticipation Securities) are available on some stocks. LEAPS are covered later in this chapter.

2. Striking Price

   Striking prices are generally spaced 2 and 1/2 points apart for stock selling at or under $25 per share, 5 points apart for stock selling at or under $200 per share and 10 points apart for stock selling over $200 per share.

Mechanics and Function of Options Clearing Corporation

An opening transaction is the initial transaction which creates an obligation of the parties, either buy or sell. The writer of an option undertakes his obligation in an "opening sale transaction," the holder in an "opening purchase transaction." The holder also agrees to pay a premium. The premium is arrived at by competitive auction bidding (open outcry) on the exchange floor. When the price has been agreed to, each party notifies the OCC which becomes the counterparty to each side of the transaction, assuming the writer's obligation and the holder's right to demand performance. Thus, while every option requires two parties, the writer and option holder, in the case of a listed option, there is no direct contractual relationship between them due to the intermediation of the OCC. The OCC pays to the writer the premium paid to it by option holder. For example, the writer of one call option (100 shares of a given stock) expiring in June with a strike price of $45 per share (a June 45 option) for a premium of $5, receives $500.

If the option holder decides to exercise the option, the OCC is notified. The OCC then selects at random a writer of the option to whom the exercise is assigned. The chosen writer must then sell or purchase the underlying stock for delivery to the option holder. If the option is allowed to expire unexercised, the writer's obligation is terminated.

FACTORS AFFECTING THE PRICE OF THE OPTION

The are six factors that affect the price of a stock option:

1. The current stock price;
2. The strike price;
3. The time to expiration;
4. The volatility of the stock price;
5. The riskfree interest rate; and
6. The dividends expected during the life of the option.

The premium an investor receives or pays for the option is a combination of all of the above factors.

Stock Price and Strike Price

The holder's profit realized on a call option increases as the price of the stock increases and becomes less valuable as the strike price increases. The reverse is true for put options; they become less valuable as the stock price increases and more valuable as the strike price increases. The difference between the stock price and strike price is referred to as the intrinsic value. The intrinsic value of an in-the-money call is the amount by which the stock price exceeds the striking price. If the call is out-of-the-money the option has a zero intrinsic value.

Time to Expiration

As the time to expiration decreases, both put and call options become less valuable. This is easily illustrated by combining two option contracts, one with 3 months remaining and one with 9 months remaining. The holder of the 9-month option has all the exercise opportunities as the holder of the 3-month option — and more. Therefore, the 9-month option must be worth at least as much as the 3-month option.

When an option is initially written, if its exercise price is close to the stock's quoted price, its value consists primarily of the time value premium. Assuming no change in the price of underlying stock, the time value diminishes as the expiration date approaches. In this regard, an option is sometimes regarded as a wasting asset. If the value of the stock remains constant, the initial value declines or wastes away.

The time value premium can be computed as follows:

Call option price + striking price − stock price

For example, DBL is trading at $112 and the March 110 call is at $3. The time value premium is $1. The intrinsic value (in-the-money) of the option is $2 ($112 − $110), therefore, the time value premium is $1.

The intrinsic value of an in-the-money option tends to reduce and, if the stock price changes sufficiently, may completely submerge the time value. Thus, a call option with six months remaining to expiration on stock whose price is $30 with an exercise price of $30, an at-the-money option, may have a value of $6, its time value. If the stock price advances within a month to $40, the option's value may rise to $14, reflecting a time value of $4, whereas if there had been no change in the stock price, the time value may have eroded by only $1; the time value is partially "submerged." As intrinsic value increases, time value disappears, and changes in the value of the option tend more to match changes in the price of the underlying stock. A similar phenomenon occurs where a put option goes deep into the money.

Most pricing models assume a random distribution of price changes, however, and an option with a strike price at or near the stock price may be viewed as an inherently wasting asset. It is for this reason that it is not feasible to be an options "dealer" in the sense of carrying an inventory of options to be sold at a mark-up from cost. The typical options dealer, in the sense of specialist or market-maker, rarely carries unhedged options positions, and usually disposes of any positions acquired (other than those hedging investment stock) within a few minutes or hours at the longest.

The fundamental difference between exchange-traded and conventional options (options that are not traded on an exchange) is the liquidity of the former. In the case of a conventional option, the grantor can terminate his obligation only by repurchasing the option from the holder. Likewise, the holder whose position has appreciated may wish to realize his gain by selling his rights. The exercise usually involves commission expenses incident to acquiring and disposing of the stock. If the stock is unlisted, a satisfactory price may be difficult to obtain.

Either party to an exchange traded option, on the other hand, can easily liquidate his position by entering into a closing transaction. This is affected by writing or purchasing an option position offsetting the position held. The grantor can terminate his obligation by purchasing an option on the same stock with the same expiration date and strike price. This is termed a "closing purchase transaction." The grantor's gain or loss is determined by comparing the amount of the premium received in the opening sale transaction with the amount of the premium required to enter the closing purchase transaction. The OCC then offsets both positions, clearing out the grantor's obligation. Similarly, the holder closes out his position by granting an option on the same stock with the same expiration date and strike price, a "closing sale transaction." Where the premium received in the closing sale transaction exceeds the premium paid in the opening purchase transaction, the holder realizes gain in this amount.

Market terminology may sometimes be confusing. The granting of an option is often referred to as the "sale" of the option. An order to sell three XYZ July 45 contracts instructs the broker to grant options on 300 shares of XYZ stock with a $45 strike price expiring in July. Likewise, an order to buy is an order to purchase options. The position of the grantor, whether the option granted is a call or a put, is referred to as "short." Thus, a person who has written a put option holds a short put position (even though profit will result only if the stock price does not fall). Similarly, the holder's position is referred to as "long," whether the position held is a call or a put. The purchaser of a put thus holds a long put position, even though a profit will result only if the stock price declines.

LEAPS

LEAPS are listed equity options with two or more years of time remaining before expiration. In fact, LEAPS is the acronym for Long-term Equity Anticipation Securities. LEAPS can be calls or puts. The LEAPS owner has the right to purchase the underlying stock at the strike price if the owner purchases a LEAPS call, or sell the underlying stock at the strike price if the owner purchases a LEAPS put.

Like equity options, LEAPS expire on the Saturday following the third Friday of the expiration month and can be exercised at any time prior to expiration. LEAPS are quoted on a per share basis as are other listed options; however, there is no standardized striking price interval for LEAPS as there are for equity options.

Standard LEAPS contracts are for 100 shares of the underlying stock and are adjusted for stock splits and stock dividends. There are position and exercise limits, currently 8,000 contracts for liquid stock, 5,500 for less liquid stock, and 3,000 for the least liquid stock. Investors must add LEAPS and equity option positions together to determine the total position quantity.

When LEAPS have less than nine months remaining until expiration they are renamed and become an ordinary equity option on the underlying stock.

One of the most important determinants of an option's price is the volatility of the underlying stock. Changes in the volatility of the underlying stock can greatly change the price of any option. LEAPS are greatly affected by changes in the volatility of the underlying stock. The value of a LEAPS contract can change greatly even when volatility changes only a little.

Changes in interest rates and dividends will also be greater on LEAPS than on conventional equity options. The cumulative effect of an interest rate or dividend rate change over the term of the LEAPS is magnified in terms of the overall price of the option.

Most option pricing models use a risk-free interest rate to price the interest component of equity options. When the term of the option is short, three to six months, the risk that interest rates will move substantially is small. However, given the two year or more period for LEAPS, the interest component can be a substantial factor in pricing the LEAPS. Additionally, choosing a two-year risk-free interest can be difficult, and LEAPS that may seem to be priced cheaply may turn out to be expensive if interest rates rise.

Dividends are another important component that can alter the price of the LEAPS. Increased dividends will have the effect of decreasing the LEAPS call price. The reason for this is that the stock price will be decreased by a greater amount when the stock goes ex-dividend.

Ex-dividend is the process whereby a stock's price is reduced when the dividend is paid. The ex-dividend date is the date on which the price reduction takes place. Investors who own stock on the ex-date will receive the dividend and those who are short stock must pay the dividend.

Dividend increases will have the opposite effect on puts. An increase in the dividend rate on the underlying common shares will cause the put to increase in price.

TAXATION

In discussing the taxation of transactions in options, it is important to understand that the grantor of an option, while burdened with a contingent legal obligation to sell or purchase stock is treated as holding an "interest in personal property," the value of which (premium received less premium required for a closing purchase) varies from day to day.

Basic Tax Definitions

A "listed" option means any option (not including stock warrants) that is traded on, or subject to the rules of a "qualified board or exchange." It means a national securities exchange registered with the SEC, a domestic board of trade designated as a contract market by the CFTC, or any other exchange, board or market which the IRS determines has rules similar to the above exchanges. The IRS has made such determinations with respect to two international exchanges: the Mercantile Division of the Montreal Exchange[1] and the International Futures Exchange (Bermuda).[2] The definition of a listed option is important as the taxation is governed by Section 1256, which generally provides for mark-to-market treatment at the taxpayer's year-end. Mark-to-market treatment can be described as a fictitious sale by the taxpayer for the option's fair market value. Although taxpayers receive no proceeds, they are nonetheless taxed on the increase or decrease in the value of the option. Section 1256 will be addressed later in this chapter and in subsequent chapters.

The basic Code rules governing the tax consequences of options transactions are contained in Section 1234. Section 1234(a) provides two rules that apply, generally, to the purchaser of all options to buy or sell property:

1. The character of gain or loss from the sale of an option by its holder is determined by the character, the property to which the option relates, would have in the holder's hands.

2. When an option expires unexercised, it is treated by the holder as sold, giving rise to capital or ordinary loss (determined by applying rule 1) in the amount of the premium paid for the option.

Exchange-Traded Options

In 1976, Congress enacted Section 1234(b), providing rules for the treatment of grantors of options relating to stock, securities (including stock and securities traded on a "when issued" basis), commodities, and commodity futures. Section 1234(b) provides generally that gain or loss realized by the grantor that arises from a closing transaction, i.e., one in which the grantor's obligation is terminated other than through the exercise or lapse of the option, as well as any gain on the lapse of any option, is short-term capital gain or loss. Section 1234(b) applies to both exchange-traded options and untraded options.

The 1997 Tax Relief Act changed the way gain or loss from the cancellation, lapse, expiration, or other termination of options to purchase or sell *non-actively traded property and realty* was characterized. Effective for terminations more than 30 days after August 5, 1997, such gains or losses are characterized as capital, since they are now covered by Section 1234A. See Section 1234A(1), as amended.

Under pre-1997-Act law, gain or loss from the repurchase or cancellation of and gain from the lapse of an option to purchase, or sell any non-actively traded property (e.g., a painting, or a building) was generally ordinary income or loss.

IRC Section 1234A, as amended by the 1997 Act, requires gain or loss attributable to the cancellation, lapse, expiration, or other termination of a right or obligation with respect to any property which is, or would be if acquired, considered a capital asset in the hands of the taxpayer to be treated as gain or loss from the sale of a capital asset. Before the 1997 changes, the application of Section 1234A was limited to personal property, not realty, and the definition of personal property in IRC Section 1234A referred to the definition of personal property contained in IRC Section 1092(d)(1). IRC Section 1092(d)(1) defines personal property as any personal property of a type which is actively traded. Therefore, under pre-1997-Act law, non-actively traded property was excluded from the definition of IRC Sections 1092(d)(1) and 1234A. For a transaction to give rise to capital gain, IRC Section 1222 requires a sale or exchange. Since a cancellation, lapse, expiration, or other termination did not give rise to a sale or exchange under pre-1997-Act law, the resulting gain or loss was considered ordinary.

Tax Consequences of Options Transactions

This discussion does *not* include options transactions entered into by options dealers in the course of their trade or business as market makers or specialists; i.e., the discussion is based on the assumption that the transactions are capital transactions with respect to each party.

The opening transactions described above are not taxable events to either the grantor or holder. Recognition of gain or loss is deferred until (1) the option expires unexercised, (2) the grantor terminates his obligation by entering into a closing purchase transaction, (3) the holder disposes of his rights under the option in a closing sale transaction, or (4) the option is exercised.

The discussion in this section assumes that transactions do not come within the purview of Section 1259, which was added by the 1997 Tax Relief Act. That section, which affects short sales and certain other transactions, requires taxpayers to recognize gain (but not loss) on entering into a constructive sale of any appreciated position in stock, partnership interests, or certain debt instruments. If Section 1259 applies, gain is recognized as if the position were sold or terminated at its fair market value on the date of the constructive sale. Section 1259, which is discussed further in the section on short sales, below, applies to any constructive sale after June 8, 1997. A "constructive sale" for purposes of Section 1259 includes:

- A short sale of the same or substantially identical property,

- An "offsetting" notional principal contract with respect to the same or substantially identical property,

- A futures or forward contract to deliver the same or substantially identical property, or

- Other transactions having the same effect as the above transactions.

In the event of exercise, gain or loss is recognized by the grantor in the case of a call, and by the holder in the case of a put. Unless the option relates to a futures contract, the exercise by the holder of a call or by the grantor of a put has no immediate tax consequence; gain or loss is recognized only when the stock acquired is disposed of.

Where the holder exercises a call, the basis of the stock acquired is the exercise price increased by the amount of the premium paid for the option plus any commission costs. The stock's holding period begins upon acquisition. The time the option was held is not counted. If the grantor's option is assigned, i.e., the grantor must deliver stock to the holder, the grantor's gain or loss from the transaction will be the exercise price of the stock called plus the amount of the premium received less the grantor's basis in the stock and any commissions. Such gain or loss will be short- or long-term depending on the period for which the stock was held.

Where the holder closes out a long call by a closing sale, the gain (the premium received less the premium paid for their option) is long- or short-term depending on the period for which the option was held. The gain will invariably be short-term since exchange traded options have maximum lives of nine months, unless the taxpayer is trading LEAPS. The grantor's gain or loss for exchange traded options is always short-term capital gain or loss under Section 1234(b)(1).

Where a put option is exercised, the holder, in determining gain or loss, deducts from the exercise price the amount of the premium paid. The gain is short- or long-term depending on the period for which the stock was held.

Where an exchange-traded call or put option is allowed to expire unexercised, it is treated as sold and, as indicated above, the holder recognizes a short-term capital loss in the amount of the premium paid; the grantor recognizes short-term capital gain.

Covered Calls

A covered call is a transaction where the grantor of a call option owns the stock needed to fulfill the obligation in the event the option is exercised.

> ### Example 2-1
>
> In September, DBL purchases 100 shares of LBD stock for 97 3/8 per share and grants a call option expiring in January with a strike price of 90 (a January '90 call) receiving a premium of 13 3/4.

Such an option serves two investment purposes: (1) if the stock is not called, the stock's yield is enhanced, and (2) if the stock's price declines, the premium serves to cushion any loss sustained. In exchange for these advantages, the grantor forfeits gain from advances in the price of the stock above the exercise price.

Assume that by mid-January, the stock price has fallen to 94 3/4. The grantor must decide whether to enter a closing purchase transaction or await exercise of the call. The results of each of these events would be as follows:

Assume the premium for a January '90 call is 4 3/4. If a closing transaction is elected, DBL will recognize short-term gain of: $1,375 (the premium received) less $475 (purchase premium paid) = $900. There will be unrealized loss on the stock of $262.50 less any commissions on the transaction.

If the call is exercised, the proceeds will be $9,000 paid by the holder plus $1,375, the premium received = $10,375. From this is subtracted the $9,737.50 basis of the stock for a short-term gain of $637.50 less any commissions on the transaction.

In this example, it is assumed that even though near expiration, the option retains some time value, since the premium for a January '90 call (4 3/4) is greater than the option's intrinsic value (4 1/2). For this reason, closing out the option results in lower net gain ($612.50, taking unrealized loss on the stock into account) than would be realized on exercise ($637.50).

Nonequity Options

A nonequity option is any listed option that does not qualify as an equity option. An equity option is defined in Section 1256(g)(6) as any option, whether or not listed, (1) to buy or sell stocks or (2) the value of which depends directly or indirectly on any group of stocks or a stock index provided there is not in effect a designation by the CFTC that the option contract is a non-equity option and that option contract is not on an index that the SEC or IRS has determined to be broadly based (for example, the S & P 500, Value Line, NYSE and Major Market indices). Thus, options on any such broad based indexes on which futures are traded (or on indexes which the IRS determines meet the legal qualifications for CFTC approval, such as the Computer Technology Index) are not treated as equity options.[3]

Other examples of nonequity options are listed options on commodities, foreign currencies, and options on futures contracts. Stock index options (and options on index futures) are "cash settlement" options; there is no delivery made of the actual stocks in the particular index. Instead, gain or loss upon exercise is computed on the basis of the index price and payment is made or received accordingly. Such cash settlement options are treated in all respects, for tax purposes, as if they called for delivery of the underlying stock.[4]

A special category of option is the "dealer equity option." This refers to any listed equity option which is purchased or granted by an options dealer in the normal course of his activity in dealing in options and which is listed on the board or exchange on which the dealer is registered. Such options and all nonequity options are Section 1256 contracts, which are subject to a special tax regime. Section 1256 will be discussed in future chapters.

Warrants

A stock warrant is a type of option. A warrant is an option granted by the issuer of the stock to which it pertains and usually has an expiration date one or several years from the date it is granted. Some warrants have no expiration date. Warrants are granted (or issued) for a number of purposes, but typically are granted in connection with the private placement of debentures or notes to the lender to obtain a lower interest rate than would otherwise be acceptable.

The amount of the premium received by the grantor is generally computed as the difference between the amount advanced by the lender and the amount which it would have advanced in exchange for the grantor's debt instrument had no warrants been issued. Warrants may contain somewhat complex terms and, when issued in connection with a loan placement, are usually traded apart from the debt instrument.

Many are listed on stock exchanges, but not on options exchanges. Although warrants qualify as equity options, they are excluded from the definition of "listed option" under Section 1256(g)(5). The tax consequences to the holder of a warrant are basically the same as those which apply to the holder of a call option although determining the amount of the premium paid is difficult. Also, the difference between the fair market value of stock shares when the warrant is exchanged and price paid for warrant is taxable income.

The grantor may terminate its obligation under a warrant prior to its expiration date by purchasing it from the holder. Under Section 1032(a), the issuer recognizes no gain or loss from the lapse or acquisition of a warrant.

Recapitulation of Tax Rules

To recapitulate the basic tax rules applicable to options transactions:

1. No gain or loss is recognized from an opening transaction, whether sale or purchase. This is true of all options, equity or nonequity, whether granted or purchased by a dealer or nondealer.

2. The holder of an option (meaning any option, listed or unlisted, equity or nonequity) recognizes gain or loss when: the option is allowed to expire unexercised, or when

the option is closed out in a closing sale transaction or assigned for value. The holder's rights may be transferred in certain circumstances. If the option is exercised, there is no taxable event and the premium is added to the price paid for the stock in determining its basis. Exercise of a put results in the sale of the property, and the premium is deducted from the sale price in determining the amount realized from the sale. Where an option is sold (or allowed to expire unexercised), the character of gain or loss depends on the property to which the option relates. The only equity options that would appear to be other than capital assets are dealer equity options.

The exception to the above rule is that gain or loss is recognized upon the exercise of an option on a Section 1256 contract.[5]

3. The holder of a nonequity option (meaning any listed option other than an equity option) holds a Section 1256 contract. Where the option is held at the close of the year, it is treated as if it were sold for its fair market value. Gain or loss is also recognized when an option on a Section 1256 contract is exercised. Exercise of any other kind of nonequity option does not give rise to recognition of gain or loss; the premium is added to the basis of the property purchased (or deducted from the price received for the property, in the case of a put option, in determining the amount realized). Cash settlement options (typically options on stock indexes) are treated as options to purchase or sell property.[6] These may be either equity or nonequity options, depending on the nature of the underlying stock index.

4. Grantors of equity options (other than those granted by options dealers in the course of their business of dealing in options) recognize short-term capital gain or loss upon the expiration of the options unexercised or the termination of their obligations thereunder by way of a closing transaction. The same applies to grantors of options on securities, commodities (including foreign currencies) and commodity futures. Grantors of options that are not on stock, securities, commodities or commodity futures, recognize ordinary income or loss upon the termination of the grantor's obligation (e.g., by assignment or repurchase) unless the option created an obligation with respect to actively traded personal property (e.g., foreign currency) in which case gain or loss is treated as from the sale of a capital asset. These may be nonequity (i.e., listed) or neither equity nor nonequity. For example, an option granted on a non-regulated futures contract (one traded on a foreign exchange) falls into this category. It is neither an equity nor a nonequity option, but is an option on commodity futures. Options on securities include options on stock indexes and interest rate instruments. Section 1234A characterizes as capital gain or loss any gain or loss attributable to the cancellation, lapse, expiration, or other termination of a right or obligation with respect to any property which is (or on acquisition would be) a capital asset in the hands of the taxpayer, or a Section 1256 contract which is a capital asset in the taxpayer's hands. This applies to forward sales of foreign currency, options on short-term and long-term interest rates offered by certain exchanges as well as to all commodity, stock index and futures options.

5. The foregoing rules apply to holders (but not to issuers) of stock warrants.

6. The general provisions of Section 1234(a) apply to holders of options which are neither equity options nor nonequity options, e.g., unlisted options to buy or sell property other than stock (including such options traded on exchanges that are not "qualified boards or exchanges").

7. Equity options purchased or granted by an options dealer in the course of the business of making markets in listed options are also subject to the rules relating to Section 1256 contracts.

WASH SALES AND SHORT SALE RULES

Transactions in stock and securities have long been subject to two sets of rules: the wash sale rules of Section 1091 and the short sale rules of Section 1233. These rules, combined with the tax straddle rules of Section 1092, have been established to prevent what Congress and the IRS perceive as abusive investment transactions contrived by sophisticated taxpayers to avoid or change the character of their economic gains. These rules are Congress and the IRS's response to the schemes developed to exploit deficiencies in earlier tax legislation. The tax straddle provisions are the principal subject of Chapter 6. A review of the wash and short sale rules is essential to an understanding of the considerably more complex tax straddle rules.

Wash Sales

The wash sale rules are set forth in Section 1091. A wash sale refers, generally, to a sale of property closely preceded or followed by the acquisition of identical property leaving the seller in the same position as if the sale had not taken place. Section 1091 was enacted to prevent investors from routinely selling off depreciated securities at year-end, claiming the losses as deductions, and reacquiring identical securities in the opening days of the ensuing year. Congress decided that there was simply no justification for the allowance of a deduction based on such a loss.

Section 1091(a) disallows any deduction under Section 165 for any loss claimed from the sale or other disposition of shares of stock or securities, if within a period beginning 30 days before such sale or disposition and ending 30 days after (the "61-day test period") the taxpayer has acquired "substantially identical" stock or securities. The disallowance also applies where within the 61-day period the taxpayer has entered into a contract or option to acquire such substantially identical stock or securities.

The wash sale rule does not apply if the taxpayer is a dealer in stock or securities, and the loss is sustained in a transaction made in the ordinary course of such business. Section 1091(a) includes in its definition of "stock or securities," options to acquire or sell stock or securities, and therefore, options dealers should also be excluded from the wash sale rules.

Commodity futures or foreign currency are not included in the definition of shares of stock or securities.[7]

The statute applies to a sale of stock at a loss and the acquisition of a warrant, for the same stock, during the 61-day period. This is true irrespective of the warrant's exercise price, since the warrant would constitute a "contract or option" to acquire substantially identical stock.

However, in Revenue Ruling 56-406, 1956-2 C.B. 523, the IRS ruled that Section 1091 does not apply to a stock warrant sold at a loss and the acquisition, within the 61-day period, of shares of stock to which the warrant related, since the warrant was not "substantially identical" to the stock. The ruling adds, however, where the relative values and price changes are so similar as to make the warrants fully convertible securities and therefore substantially identical with the shares of stock, the warrant would be treated as the equivalent of shares of stock substantially identical to the shares sold.

The wash sale rules come into play only when substantially identical stock or securities are acquired within the 61-day test period of the sale of stock or securities at a loss. Exercise of an option or warrant should trigger the rule, since they would constitute a purchase, but the exchange of a convertible debenture for stock would not constitute a taxable acquisition and thus would not trigger the rule.[8]

Most of the difficulty encountered in applying Section 1091 involves the determination of whether the property acquired during the 61-day period is substantially identical to the property disposed of at a loss.

How close do the terms of a debt instruments need to be before two debt instruments will be substantially identical? Assume that one bond bears a 4.5% coupon and matures in approximately 16 years for a price of approximately $8,800 for each $1,000 of principal amount, and the purchase on the same date of a bond with the same principal amount, issued by the same issuer, bearing the same coupon for the same price, but maturing approximately six months later than the bonds sold. The yield of the bond purchased is approximately .0007% lower than the bonds sold. While maturity dates (and hence, yields) of bonds sold and purchased is a factor to be considered in determining whether they were substantially identical, the difference in the yield of the bond purchased and sold is so insignificant that it should be ignored for purposes of the statute.[9] Therefore, bonds purchased would be considered substantially identical to those sold. The same reasoning was applied to the sale of bonds maturing in $20^1/_2$ years followed by the purchase of bonds identical in all other respects but maturing in 23 years, both of which were callable at any time after a certain date. The redemption feature apparently overrides any effect the difference in maturity dates have. Where an investor holding the debt security sold would, from the standpoint of his investment objectives, be indifferent to their replacement by the securities purchased, the securities will be considered identical.[10]

Where a taxpayer sells bonds at a loss and then simultaneously purchases for the same price, bonds nearly identical in all respects (principal amount, coupon, maturity and call date) except that they were issued by a different issuer, the court will consider the identity of the issuer (which influences the element of risk). Unless there is a relation between the issuers where a default by one such bank would give a holder of its obligations a claim against the other for the full unpaid balance of the defaulted obligation, the risk differential will prevent the bonds from being substantially identical.[11]

Generally, the words substantially identical indicate that something less than precise correspondence will suffice to make the transaction a wash sale. However, how much less will depend on whether the taxpayer's economic position has been changed. The new position must differ from the old in a way that has an impact on the taxpayer's investment goals and objectives, or the risk/reward components, viewed objectively.

Decisive factors would seem to include: identity of the issuer, the security's yield, redemption provisions and the security's maturity date (where significant). In terms of investment terminology, there would seem to be no wash sale where the substitution of the securities purchased for those sold would affect the duration of the taxpayer's investment position. For example, an interest bearing bond would never be substantially identical to a zero coupon bond, nor would, generally, any bond the value of which is more sensitive to interest rate fluctuations than the bond sold.

The question of whether stock (and/or stock rights) may be substantially identical to other stock is discussed below in the analysis of the short sale rules. It should be noted, however, that the IRS has ruled that where stock is sold at a loss and the taxpayer within the 61-day period grants a deep-in-the-money put option which is virtually certain to be exercised by the holder, he will be deemed to have entered into a contract to purchase the stock.[12]

The following examples illustrate statutory provisions described above:

Example 2–2

The taxpayer (T) sells a bond having a basis of $1,000 on December 15 for $750, realizing a $250 loss. On January 5, he acquires an identical bond for $755. He is in virtually the same position as he was before. However, his investment in the bond has increased to $1,005. In essence, the $110 loss sustained is not a true economic loss, and is not recognizable for tax purposes. The same result would occur if the taxpayer enters into a similar transaction involving stock. For example, T holds a share of stock with a basis of $1,000 on December 15. The price of the stock has fallen to $750. On the same day, T purchases a call option on the same stock expiring in 45 days with an exercise price of $800 for a premium of $6. On December 28, T sells the stock for $800, realizing a $200 loss. On January 5, T exercises the call. T is in the same position as if the stock had never been disposed of other than having had to expend $6 for the option premium. In these circumstances, the $200 loss from the sale of the stock is disallowed (T's basis in the stock received from the exercise of the call is increased by the $6 premium).

Example 2–3

Assume that T, for a premium of $2,500 ($25 a share), purchases an option to buy 100 shares of XYZ stock for $50 per share at a time when the stock price is $74. The option expires in 60 days. It has virtually no time value (since the $25/share premium exceeds the price spread by only $1). The stock price falls to $70, at which time T sells the option for $2,050. Within the 61-day period after selling the option, A purchases 100 shares of XYZ stock. Given the above, even though a stock option is not substantially identical to the stock to which it relates (but may be substantially identical to another option relating to the same stock), the IRS may take the view that the option, because it is so deep in the money, could be considered as a position in the stock.

Example 2–4

The taxpayer (T) on November 1 purchases call options on 500 shares of ABC stock with an exercise price of $85 expiring the following January. The price of ABC on that date is $102. The premium paid for the options is $20 1/4; the total premium paid is thus $10,125. On December 1, the stock price has fallen to $98. T sells the options for a premium of $15 per share, a total of $7,500, sustaining a loss of $2,625. On December 15, the stock price has risen to $105. On that date, A purchases another 500 January 85 options for a premium of $21 3/4 per share, a total of $10,875. In these circumstances, it is somewhat unclear whether the wash sale rule will apply, since the options acquired have a different time to expiration than the options sold. However, the IRS would probably disallow the loss since the difference in the time value of the options sold and those purchased is relatively insignificant when compared to their intrinsic values.

If the wash sale rule applies, the holding period of the security disposed of is tacked onto that of the replacement security.[13] In determining the holding period of stock or securities whose acquisition (or contract or option to acquire) triggered the wash sale rule, the holding period of the stock or securities sold or disposed of is added to that of the acquired property.

Example 2–5

Assume that a share of stock held for 10 months is sold at a loss and that an option to acquire a share of substantially identical stock is acquired within the 61-day period. The 10-month holding period is not tacked to the holding period of the option. Assume that the option is exercised 3 months after its acquisition. The holding period of an option is not tacked to the holding period of stock acquired by exercise of the option. However, under Section 1223(4), the 10-month holding period of the stock sold is tacked to that of the stock acquired by exercising the option.

Under Section 1091(d), where a security or share of stock (or call option) is purchased, and such purchase triggers the wash sale rule, the basis of the property acquired is its cost plus the disallowed loss.

Example 2–6

If there is a wash sale of a bond with a basis of $100 for $80, followed by the purchase of a replacement bond for $90, the taxpayer is out of pocket a total of $110. Therefore, the basis of the new property is equal to the basis of the old property ($100), increased by $10, the disallowed loss.

The basis rule is the same even if the acquisition of an option is the triggering event.

Example 2–7

The basis of stock sold is $1,000, sale price $800, cost of option $10, exercise price of option $800. The option will have a basis of $210. If the option is exercised, the $210 basis is added to the purchase price of the stock. If the option expires unexercised, the loss allowed is the $210 basis.

The wash sale rules have specific rules where different blocks of stock are acquired at different times, but sold at the same time.

Example 2–8

Assume that A purchased 100 shares of ABC for $100 per share, a second 100 share block for $75 per share and a third block of 100 shares for $50 per share. Subsequently, A sells 250 shares for $80 each, delivering the shares in the same order purchased. A has a $2,000 loss from the shares with a basis of $100, a $500 gain from those with a $75 basis, and a $1,500 gain from the 50 shares with a $50 basis. If within 30 days from the date of that transaction, A purchases another 250 shares of ABC stock, the $2,000 loss on the $100 basis stock cannot be used to offset the $2,000 gain from the sale of the other 150 shares.

Where the amount of stock or securities acquired (or covered by contract or option) is less than the amount sold or otherwise disposed of, the regulations provide rules for matching the acquired and disposed of property. Similarly, where the amount of stock and securities acquired is not less than the amount sold or disposed of, the regulations provide matching rules.[14]

Example 2–9

If five XYZ debentures having a basis of $10,000 are sold for $9,670 each (a loss of $330 per debenture) and within the 61 day period two identical debentures are acquired, only 40% or $660 of the total loss of $1,650 on the sale of the five debentures is disallowed.[15]

Example 2–10

A holds 3 shares of XYZ stock having bases, respectively, of $100, $90 and $80 acquired, respectively, in 1991, 1992 and 1993. On March 15, 1994, A sells the shares with bases of $80 and $100 for $70 each, and he sells the share with a $90 basis on March 31, 1994 for $65. On April 5, 1994, A purchases one share of XYZ for $65.

If A can establish the order in which the shares sold on March 15 were disposed of, the wash sale rule is applied to disallow only the loss on the share first sold. If the order cannot be determined, the first acquired (the share purchased in 1991) is presumed to be the first sold.

If on April 6, A had purchased another share of XYZ, this acquisition would be matched with the second share disposed of in order of time (or presumed time).

If on April 5, instead of acquiring only one share of XYZ, A had acquired two shares, and on April 6 had acquired two more shares, the shares acquired would be matched with the shares disposed of in order of time. That is, the April 5 acquisitions would be matched with the shares having a basis of $80 and $100, and the first acquired (if this can be determined) April 6 acquisition would be matched with the $90 basis share sold on March 31.

A special wash sale rule, contained in Section 860F(d), applies to residual interests in Real Estate Mortgage Investment Conduits (REMICs). REMICs are considered "securities" for purposes of the wash sale rules. Further, except as may be provided in regulations, any residual interest in a REMIC and any other such interest (or interest in a taxable mortgage pool comparable to a REMIC residual interest) are treated as substantially identical securities. A residual interest in a REMIC has an extended test-period, i.e., the loss is disallowed if another such interest is acquired within 6 months before or after the date the disposition giving rise to the loss.

SHORT SALES

The purpose of the short sale rules is to prevent the manipulation of holding periods, and, in the case of Section 1259 (which was added by the 1997 Tax Relief Act) to require recognition where a taxpayer has entered into a transaction that eliminates substantially all of the risk of loss and opportunity for income or gain with respect to an appreciated financial position. The rules are intended to prevent the following abuses:

1. Extending the holding period of appreciated stock and futures positions to obtain the preferential long-term capital gain rate without incurring the risk associated with the stock's price movement, and

2. The conversion of loss from long-term to short-term.

3. The postponement of gain recognition where a constructive sale has occurred.

A short sale is an arrangement under which the seller sells a security in the market and is then obligated to make delivery of a security at some date in the future. The short seller may or may not own the security he intends to sell. If the short seller owns securities identical to those sold short, the sale is said to be "against the box."

Assuming the rules of Section 1259 do not apply, recognition of gain or loss occurs at the time the sale is closed, i.e., when the seller makes delivery of the security. If during the period the short sale is open (after the sale and before delivery) the security goes down in value, the short seller will realize a gain. Alternatively, if the security increases in value, the short seller will realize a loss. Gain or loss from closing the sale is, therefore, the difference between the amount realized from the sale of the borrowed security and the cost of the security used to close the sale.

The usual form of a short sale is as follows:

1. The seller borrows the security to be sold from a broker;

2. The borrowed security is immediately sold on the open market;

3. The borrower/seller undertakes an obligation to return the identical security to the lender;

4. The short sale is closed when the security is delivered to the lender.[16]

The short seller is entitled to any income paid while in the broker's hands. When a dividend is paid on the borrowed stock prior to the date the short sale is closed, the short seller must pay to the buyer an equivalent amount in lieu of such dividend. Similarly, where an interest bearing instrument is borrowed for use in a short sale, the short seller must make an interest payment to the lender in lieu of the interest the lender would have received had he held the bond.

A short sale is a way to speculate on downward price movements or to hedge against such movements with respect to securities held by the seller. Short sales are often used by securities dealers for speculation, hedging and arbitrage. In such a case, where the property used to close the sale consists of securities held in inventory, the short sale rules do not apply. They apply only where the property used to close the short sale is a capital asset.[17]

The discussion in this section assumes that transactions do not come within the purview of Section 1259, which was added by the 1997 Tax Relief Act. That section, which affects short sales and certain other transactions, requires taxpayers to recognize gain (but not loss) on entering into a constructive sale of any appreciated position in stock, partnership interests, or certain debt instruments. If Section 1259 applies, gain is recognized as if the position were sold or terminated at its fair market value on the date of the constructive sale. Section 1259 applies to any constructive sale after June 8, 1997. A "constructive sale" for purposes of Section 1259 includes:

- A short sale of the same or substantially identical property,

- An "offsetting" notional principal contract with respect to the same or substantially identical property,

- A futures or forward contract to deliver the same or substantially identical property, or

- Other transactions having the same effect as the above transactions.

A short sale against the box is similar to writing a covered call option; however, there are differences in the expected risks and returns. Whether to sell short or write a covered call will depend on sometimes widely varying investment goals and strategies.

Example 2–11

Assume that short seller A owns 100 shares of XYZ stock with a basis of $20 a share. The current price is $50. A sells 100 shares short, realizing $5,000 on the sale of the borrowed stock. The price increases to $70. A has suffered a $2,000 loss which he would have realized had the short sale not have been entered into. Should the price continue to rise, A can close the sale. A has locked in $30 of gain and is shut out from profiting from any appreciation in the stock's value while the short sale is open. If the stock price falls, A realizes $100 of gain for every $1 the price falls below $50, for a potential maximum of $50,000.

Example 2–12

Assume A writes a covered call with a strike price of $50, receiving a premium of $10. The stock price goes to $70. If it is called away, A forfeits any profit from the stock's appreciation and realizes net gain of $40, including the premium. Should the stock price remain at $50 or fall, A's maximum profit is $10.

Note that the advent of Section 1259 may change the tax result in the foregoing example. The short sale rules apply to stocks and securities (including stocks and securities dealt with on a "when issued" basis), and commodity futures which are capital assets in the taxpayer's hands.[18]

The definition does not include commodities, entering into a short futures or forward sale position while holding a physical commodity (or its acquisition thereafter) does not come within the short sale rules.

COORDINATION WITH WASH SALE RULE

A short sale can be analyzed as involving two sales: (1) the sale of the borrowed securities and (2) the closing of the short sale by delivery of identical securities to the securities borrowed to the lender. For tax purposes, insofar as the short seller is concerned, there has been no sale until the closing; until that time, no particular share of stock has been appropriated to the closing transaction.

The regulations provide that where box stock is used to close a short sale against the box, the wash sale rule is applied by treating the date the short sale was entered into as the date of sale.[19] The wash sale provisions apply where the replacement stock is purchased (or the taxpayer acquires an option or contractual right to purchase such stock) within 30 days of entering into the short sale. The wash sale provisions apply to any loss realized from closing a short sale if within a period beginning 30 days before and ending 30 days after such closing (1) substantially identical stock or securities are sold, or (2) another short sale of substantially identical stock or securities is entered into.[20]

Example 2–13

On September 1, A holds a share of XYZ stock with a basis of $100. The price declines to $80. A enters into a short sale, selling the borrowed share at that price. On the same day, A purchases a share of XYZ for $80. A waits for 31 days and closes the short sale with the $100 basis stock sustaining a loss of $20. Without the regulatory rule, the wash sale provisions do not apply since the $80 basis stock was acquired more than 30 days from the date the $100 basis stock was disposed of at a loss. Under the regulations, the disposition of the $100 basis stock is deemed to have occurred on the date the short sale was entered into, and the wash sale rule applies to disallow the loss.

Example 2–14

A holds a share of XYZ stock with a basis of $100 (the $100 stock). On November 1, A enters into a short sale against the box selling a borrowed share of stock for $105. On December 23, the stock price has advanced to $120. At that point, A has unrealized gain on the $100 stock of $20 and unrealized loss on the short sale of $15. A closes the short sale with a share purchased for $120 (the $120 stock) realizing a loss of $15. The wash sale rules would disallow the $15 loss, the loss is added to the basis of the retained $100 stock. Thus, if that stock is later sold for $120, there is only $5 of gain.

Short-Term Gains and Holding Periods

There are three basic short sale rules:[21]

The first rule,[22] provides that if on the date of a short sale securities substantially identical to the securities sold short have not been held by the taxpayer long-term, or if "substantially identical" property is acquired after the short sale while it is still open, any gain from the closing of the short sale is treated as short-term gain.

The second rule,[23] provides that the holding period of the substantially identical securities property is treated as beginning on the date the short sale is closed.

The third rule[24] was enacted to prevent the conversion of long-term loss to short-term loss. Under this rule, if on the date of a short sale of property, the taxpayer has held substantially identical property long-term, then any loss from the closing of the short sale is long-term loss. This rule prevents the taxpayer from closing the short sale with property purchased for that purpose and claiming a short-term loss in circumstances where the short sale, in effect, protected against erosion in the value of the securities held long-term. This rule applies to losses only.

Payments Made in Connection with Short Sales

The proceeds from the sale of the borrowed stock or securities are generally held by the borrower's or lender's broker as security for performance of the seller's obligation to return them. The seller may free the funds by posting collateral with the broker securing performance. In some cases, the broker holding cash collateral will pay the seller a rebate on the funds or other collateral held while the sale remains open. The rebate will approximate the interest that would be paid on a loan in the same amount as the sale proceeds. These payments should be generally reportable as ordinary interest income and deductible as interest by the broker under Section 162.

The borrower is obliged to pay to the lender an amount equal to all dividends distributed with respect to the stock while the short sale remains open. In the case of debt instruments, similar payments are made to the lender in lieu of any interest payments due. Such payments are, as a general rule, deductible by the borrower either under Section 162 as a business expense (if the borrower is a trader or dealer) or under Section 212 as an investment expense (if the borrower is an investor). It should be noted that the deduction of Section 212 expenses may be limited. Since these payments have some of the characteristics of amounts paid for the use of money, deductions for the payments made by an investor are subject to the limitation on the amount of investment interest that is deductible for any taxable year. Section 163(d)(3)(C) provides that for purposes of determining the amount of investment interest, there is included any amount allowed as a deduction in connection with personal property used in a short sale. The deduction for investment interest is limited to net investment income. The amount of any deduction allowed to an investor is not subject to the floor on miscellaneous itemized deductions.[25] In the case of a trader or dealer, the deduction is not itemized and not subject to the investment interest limitation.

The IRS has characterized amounts paid by the borrower of stock to the lender with respect to nontaxable stock dividends and liquidating distributions are treated as capital expenditures and are, therefore, not deductible.[26]

Where an "in lieu of dividend" payment is made with respect to the borrowed stock and the short sale is closed within 45 days after it was entered into, no deduction is allowed; the amount of such payment(s) is added to the basis of the stock used to close the short sale.[27] In the case of an "extraordinary dividend," the sale must be held open for 1 year in lieu of 45 days for the payment to be deductible.[28]

Where the "in lieu of dividend" payment is not deductible because of failure to hold the sale open for at least 45 days, the amount of the payment added to the basis of the stock used to close the short sale is reduced by the amount of any rebates paid by the broker holding the sale proceeds (or other collateral) that is includible by the borrower as ordinary income. This offset does not apply in the case of extraordinary dividends.[29]

ENDNOTES

[1] Rev. Rul. 86-7, 1986-1 C.B. 295.

[2] Rev. Rul. 85-72, 1985-21 C.B. 286.

[3] See, Rev. Rul. 86-6, 1986-1 C.B. 295 and Section 1256(g)(6)(B).

[4] See, Section 1234(c)(2).

[5] Section 1234(c)(1).

[6] Section 1234(c)(2).

[7] See, Rev. Rul. 71-568, 1971-2 C.B. 312; Rev. Rul. 74-218, 1974-1 C.B. 202.

[8] Section 1091(a).

[9] Hanlin v. Commr., 108 F.2d 429 (3d Cir. 1939), aff'g 38 B.T.A. 811 (1938), nonacq. 1939-1 C.B. (Part 1) 55.

[10] Id.

[11] Id.

[12] Rev. Rul. 85-87, 1985-1 C.B. 268.

[13] See, Section 1223(4).

[14] See, Section 1091(b) and (c) and Regs. Section 1.1091-1(c) and (d). Regs. provide that matching is to be done on the basis of the order of acquisition.

[15] Regs. Section 1.1091-1(b).

[16] Regs. Section 1.12331(a)(1).

[17] Section 1233(a); Regs. Section 1.12331(a)(2).

[18] Section 1233(e)(2)(A).

[19] Regs. Section 1.10911(g).

[20] Section 1091(e).

[21] See, Sections 1233(b)(1), 1233(b)(2) and 1233(d).

[22] 1233(b)(1).

[23] 1233(b)(2).

[24] 1233(d).

[25] See, Section 67(b)(9).

[26] Rev. Rul. 72521, 19722 C.B. 178.

[27] Section 263(h)(1).

[28] Section 263(h)(2).

[29] Section 263(h)(5).

CHAPTER 3

FUTURES, FORWARDS, AND OTHER DERIVATIVE PRODUCTS

OBJECTIVE

After completing this chapter you will understand:

- The basic uses of futures, forwards, and other derivative products.

- The basic economic and financial aspects of these derivative products.

- The basic tax principles relating to these products.

INTRODUCTION

The discussion in this section assumes that transactions do not come within the purview of Section 1259, which was added by the 1997 Tax Relief Act. That section, which affects short sales and certain other transactions, requires taxpayers to recognize gain (but not loss) on entering into a constructive sale of any appreciated position in stock, partnership interests, or certain debt instruments. If Section 1259 applies, gain is recognized as if the position were sold or terminated at its fair market value on the date of the constructive sale. Section 1259 applies to any constructive sale after June 8, 1997. A "constructive sale" for purposes of Section 1259 includes:

- A short sale of the same or substantially identical property,

- An "offsetting" notional principal contract with respect to the same or substantially identical property,

- A futures or forward contract to deliver the same or substantially identical property, or

- Other transactions having the same effect as the above transactions.

The primary economic function of the futures market is hedging. Hedging can be described as taking a position to offset the risk of actually owning the physical commodity or financial instrument. For example, stock index futures offset the risk of owning stocks. A portfolio manager who manages a large portfolio of stocks could sell index futures to offset the price movement in the stock market. This may have the effect of offsetting much of the price risk of the stock portfolio. Also, he is able to establish the hedge at a lower cost than selling short the portfolio. Hedging allows the portfolio manager to be more efficient in his pricing and hence, more profitable.

Futures and forwards can also be used to hedge foreign currency. For example, assume a U.S. business obtains a large contract to supply a Swiss manufacturer. The manufacturer wishes to pay in Swiss francs but the payment is not due for six months. The profit of the U.S. business will be greater if the Swiss francs are worth more dollars in six months and less if the Swiss francs are worth fewer dollars in six months. In bidding on the contract the U.S. business could have incorporated the cost of hedging the currency risk. The U.S. business is long Swiss francs, i.e., they will receive Swiss francs in six months. To protect against the risk that the value of the Swiss franc will decline, the U.S. business could sell short a Swiss franc futures contract that expires in six months. This will allow the U.S. business to lock in the profit from the contract. The same could have been accomplished with a foreign currency forward. Futures and forwards provide the investor with a way to offset business risks associated with movements in the physical commodities they manufacture, interest rates and foreign currency. Without the ability to hedge business would be unable to control these risks. The discussion that follows will hopefully provide some insight into how this is done.

FUTURES

A futures contract is an agreement between two parties to buy or sell an asset (a commodity or financial asset), at a certain time in the future for a certain price. Futures contracts are traded on an exchange. The largest exchanges on which futures contracts are traded are the Chicago Board of Trade (CBOT) and the Chicago Mercantile Exchange (CME). On these exchanges, a very wide range of commodity futures contracts are offered: aluminum, cattle, copper, gold, lumber, pork bellies, sugar, tin and wool. Also offered are a wide range of futures contracts on financial products: stock indices, currencies, Treasury bills and bonds.

To maintain an orderly market, the exchange specifies certain standard features of the contract. The exchange also guarantees that the terms of the contract are honored. A futures contract has an exact delivery date. The specific contract is referred to by that date and the exchange specifies the period during which delivery is required. The exchange also specifies the amount of the asset to be delivered, the quality and the delivery location. The exchange also places limits on the amount by which the futures price can move in any one day.

The vast majority of futures transactions are closed out through the purchase of an offsetting position. For instance, if one is long one July corn futures contract, he can close out the position by shorting the same July corn contract. Delivery of the underlying asset is quite rare, although it does occur.

There are two types of traders in the trading pits on the floor of an exchange: commission brokers, who execute trades for other people for a commission; and locals, who trade for their own account.

Futures prices are generally quoted in a convenient, easily understandable way and the minimum movement in a futures contract is consistent with the way the price is quoted. For example, crude oil futures on the New York Mercantile (NYMEX) are quoted in dollars per barrel to the nearest penny. The minimum price movement in the futures contract is one cent per barrel.

For most contracts, there is a limit to the amount per day that the contract can fluctuate. For example, assume the limit on the daily price movement of the crude oil contract on the NYMEX is $1. If the price moves up $1 (limit up), or $1 down (limit down), during the day, trading will be halted for the day. The exchange has the authority to step in to change the limits.

To ensure against defaults in contracts, investors are required to deposit funds to cover changes in the price of the contract. This deposit is called margin. When the investor first enters into a futures contract, the broker determines the margin requirement — although minimum levels are determined by the exchange. At the end of the trading day the margin account is adjusted to reflect the investor's gain or loss. A maintenance margin is set, usually at a level lower than the initial margin (75% of initial margin). When the investor's balance in the margin account falls below the maintenance margin, the investor will receive a margin call, requiring him to increase the amount in the margin account to the initial margin level.

For example, assume the investor purchases a contract calling for the delivery of gold (100 ounces) at $400. Assume the margin is $2,000 per contract and the maintenance margin is $1,500. Further, assume that the value of the contract has declined to $398. The investor has a loss of $200 ($2/oz. * 100 ozs.). The balance in the margin account will be decreased by $200. The broker's account with the exchange will be debited $200, i.e., the broker is required to pay, at the end of the trading day, $200. The exchange will pass the amount on to the broker with the short position. If the contract further declines to $394, the investor will receive a margin call of $600, the difference between the initial margin and the value in the margin account (variation margin). If the investor does not provide the variation margin, the broker will sell out the contract.

Some financial futures are settled in cash. This is because it is impossible or inconvenient to deliver the underlying asset. For instance, a future on the S&P 500 stock index would require delivery of all 500 stocks in the index. When a contract is settled in cash, the contract is marked-to-market on the last trading day (or the opening price on the day after) and all positions are considered closed.

FUTURES PRICING

As the contract gets closer to the delivery month, the price of the futures contract approaches the new spot price of the underlying asset. This is so because a futures contract is priced at the spot on the issue date increased for an interest charge. When the delivery date is reached, the futures contract has lost the interest component and therefore equals the current spot price. Simply put, a futures pricing is based on the spot price of the commodity at the time the contract is offered adjusted by the interest and carrying charges.[1]

TAXATION OF FUTURES CONTRACTS

Generally

U.S. futures contracts are required to be traded on and regulated by an exchange. A regulated futures contract (RFC) is considered a Section 1256 contract.

A Section 1256 contract is an instrument requiring recognition for tax purposes of gain or loss at year-end. Section 1256 contracts are marked to market and the gain or loss is treated as 60% long-term and 40% short-term capital gain or loss.[2]

Each contract is treated as if it were sold for its fair market value on the last day of the taxpayer's taxable year. The mark-to-market and 60/40 treatment also applies to the termination or transfer of the taxpayer's rights or obligations under a Section 1256 contract.[3]

Regulated Futures Contract

A regulated futures contract is a futures contract which is required to be collateralized on a mark-to-market basis and which is traded on or subject to the rules of a qualified board or exchange.[4] A qualified board or exchange includes a national securities exchange which is registered with the SEC; a domestic board of trade designated as a contract maker by the CFTC, or other exchange, board of trade, or other market which the Secretary of the Treasury designates as a qualified board or exchange.[5] All futures contracts traded in the U.S. must be traded on a board or exchange regulated by the CFTC.[6] Hence, all domestically traded futures contracts are regulated futures contracts.

To date, the only non-U.S. exchanges to elect to be designated as a qualified board or exchange are the Mercantile Division of the Montreal Exchange and the International Futures Exchange Ltd. (Bermuda).[7] All other foreign exchanges do not qualify. If the contract is traded under the Mutual Offset System between the CME and the SIMEX, the contract will be treated on the exchange where it is assumed (i.e., where it clears) rather than where it is executed. Thus, where the CME is the origination exchange and the SIMEX is the execution exchange and the contract is assumed by the CME, the contract will be a Section 1256 contract.[8]

Foreign Currency Contracts

Certain foreign currency contracts can be Section 1256 contracts. A foreign currency contract is a contract which requires delivery of or the settlement depends on a foreign currency. If the foreign currency is one in which positions are also traded through RFCs and the foreign currency contract is traded on the interbank market and is entered into at arm's length at a price determined by reference to the price in the interbank market, the contract will qualify as a Section 1256 contract. A contract traded through a futures commission merchant is considered traded through the interbank market.

Foreign currency contracts are Section 988 contracts.[9] Section 988 does not address the timing of recognition of gains and losses, but only the character. Therefore, the resulting gain or loss of a foreign currency contract under Section 988 is ordinary,[10] rather than 60/40 long-term/short-term capital gain. If a foreign currency contract is both Section 988 and Section 1256 contracts, the taxpayer can make an election under Section 988 to treat the gain or loss as capital.[11] Otherwise, foreign currency contracts that are both Section 988 and Section 1256 contracts will be marked to market at year end and the gain or loss will be ordinary.[12] The election is made on an instrument-by-instrument basis.[13] Note that the 1997 Tax Relief Act added an exception to the Section 988 rules for small (gain of $200 or less) personal foreign currency transactions, effective after 1997.

If a Section 1256 contract is part of a hedging transaction the mark-to-market and 60/40 rules will not apply if the taxpayer elects out of Section 1256 by clearly identifying such transaction as a hedging transaction.[14]

FORWARDS

Forward sales contracts call for delivery of a specified quantity of tangible goods at a specified future date. They differ from futures contracts in that they are generally not standardized and are not traded on any domestic exchanges or boards of trade. Such transactions are commonly entered into to hedge risks from exposure to foreign currency rate fluctuation, in which case they are contracts to purchase or sell units of a specified currency. Usually, they are entered into with the foreign exchange department of a bank located in a major money market, or between such a bank and a foreign bank.

Margin, if any, depends to a large degree on the parties' credit and (sometimes) customer status. There is no fixed regulatory minimum, nor is there a mark-to-market system as in the case of futures.

Much like futures contracts, the rights and obligations of a party to a forward sales contract may be terminated by delivery of the underlying asset, or closed out by cancellation or the acquisition of an offsetting contract. When the contract is settled through other than delivery of the underlying asset, the profiting party will receive a cash payment from the other contracting party. Gain or loss will depend on whether the currency exchange rate has moved favorably or unfavorably to the contract holder.

FORWARD PRICING

Forwards are priced similar to futures. The price of the forward is computed by adjusting the spot price of the commodity at the time the contract is offered for interest and carrying charges. In fact, in some markets the spot price is calculated off the forward price, that is, interest and carrying charges are backed out of the forward price to determine the current spot price.

TAXATION OF FORWARD CONTRACTS

Most forward sale and purchase agreements relating to major currencies are traded on the interbank market, in which case they are Section 1256 contracts. In some cases the contract will reflect:

1. Interest rates other than those established by the interbank market;

2. Currencies other than the major ones, or

3. Odd or extraordinarily deep maturity dates.

Where this is the case, they will not be considered to be traded on the interbank market and will not be Section 1256 contracts. The rules of Section 1256 contracts are discussed later in this chapter.

Gain or loss on forward contracts, which are not Section 1256 contracts, is recognized when the rights and obligations under contract are terminated, either through delivery, offset, or cash settlement.

Economically, forward contracts have many features in common with futures. However, one important tax distinction is that they are not subject to the short sale rules of Section 1233. Section 1233 applies only to short sales involving stocks, securities and commodity futures (not the commodities themselves). Short sales were discussed briefly in Chapter 2.

FUTURES OPTIONS

Options on futures contracts are traded in a number of futures contract markets. These options provide significantly different risks and rewards from the underlying futures contracts themselves. The purchaser of an option assumes no risk beyond the premium paid. The grantor, while exposed to substantially greater risk, can always terminate such exposure in a closing purchase transaction.

The grantor of a futures option undertakes, in consideration of the premium received, to enter into a futures contract. In this case, the grantor of a long call option agrees, upon exercise of the call, to enter into a futures contract at the agreed on strike (futures) price. The exercising option holder acquires the offsetting short futures position at that price. In the case of a long put, the grantor agrees to enter into a short contract with the exercising holder acquiring the offsetting long futures position. The grantor, after making payment of margin reflecting the difference between the strike price and the current futures price, may immediately close out his position or continue to hold it in the hope that the futures price will move favorably, enabling him to recoup part of his loss.

TAXATION OF OPTIONS ON FUTURES

Section 1234(c)(1) provides that gain or loss must be recognized on the exercise of an option on a Section 1256 contract. Hence, the net gain or loss (i.e., the amount credited to the exercising holder of a long call where the futures price has risen less the premium paid for the option or the amount required to be paid by the grantor of the short call less the premium received) of the grantors and holders of the futures options must be recognized at the time of exercise irrespective of whether they elect to retain the long or short futures position acquired or to close such positions out at the time of exercise.

If the option is not exercised but is allowed to lapse or is closed out prior to exercise, the gain or loss arising on lapse or on the closing transaction is treated as capital gain or loss, if the underlying commodity would be a capital asset in the hands of the taxpayer, and an ordinary loss if the underlying commodity would be an ordinary asset.

Under Section 1234A(1), gain or loss from the cancellation, lapse or other expiration of a right or obligation with respect to personal property (including all actively traded personal property) which is or would be a capital asset in the hands of the taxpayer is treated as gain or loss from the sale of a capital asset. Therefore, the gain or loss from forward contracts for currency or securities is not dependent on the manner in which the holder of the contract elects to terminate his rights or obligations.

Example 3-1

DBL, for a premium of $X, grants a call option in January on a futures contract that requires November delivery of 10,000 units of commodity C at a price of $1 per unit. If the call is exercised, and the exercise is assigned to DBL by the clearing organization, DBL must enter into a short futures contract with the same price. The holder exercising the option acquires an offsetting long position. DBL may immediately close out the contract acquired through the clearing organization, making payment of an amount equal to the difference between the strike price and the futures price on the date the short position was acquired and disposed of. Assuming that the price has moved to $1.10 per unit, DBL must immediately post $1,000 with the clearing organization upon acquiring the short position. DBL realizes loss on the difference between this amount and the premium received whether or not the position acquired is closed out. If the position is closed out on the same date, there is no further gain or loss. Of course, DBL may retain the short position after posting the required margin. If the price subsequently moves to $1.05, he will have recouped $500 of the margin posted, and may then close out the position. If DBL closes the position, he must recognize the $500 gain realized at this time.

Under the rules of Section 1256, the grantor or holder of a futures option who holds such an option on the last business day of the year must treat the position as if it were sold for its fair market value and recognize any gain or loss. Such gain or loss is then taken into account to adjust any gain or loss resulting from the disposition, exercise or termination of the option position.

INTEREST RATE INSTRUMENTS

Various types of corporate debt obligations are traded on domestic and foreign exchanges as well as on the over-the-counter market. The over-the-counter market covers all transactions not occurring on an exchange. The participants in this market are primarily dealers, some of whom are market makers in one or more issues, who purchase and sell securities as principals, deriving income from marking up the securities sold. Most transactions on exchanges are affected by brokers acting as agents for the seller. OTC market makers and brokers who represent customers must register with the SEC and become members of the National Association of Securities Dealers (NASD). Transactions can be conducted by telephone or computer terminal. Obligations issued by the U.S. Treasury, so-called Agency issues, and obligations issued by states and municipalities are traded exclusively on the over-the-counter market. Contracts and obligations relating to foreign currency are traded in the interbank market.

Regular and residual REMIC interests (see Chapter 8 for a discussion on REMICs), mortgage backed securities, collateralized mortgage obligations, certificates of deposit, commercial paper, and securities collateralized by credit card receivables or automobile dealer paper are traded over-the-counter.

TREASURY AND AGENCY ISSUES

The Treasury Department periodically issues negotiable debt instruments. These are usually bought up by bond dealers who resell them to banks, financial institutions, and to the general public. Sales to the general public are usually made by brokers at a mark-up.

Treasury bills (T-bills) are short-term obligations maturing in one year or less. They are issued at discount and bear no interest coupon. The interest earned by the holder is the difference between the price paid and the amount payable at maturity. Given a situation in which there is no change in prevailing short-term interest rates, the value of the bill will increase each day to maturity. If rates rise, the value will decrease; if they fall, the value will increase. Thus, the value of a T-bill as of any point in time subsequent to its issue will depend both on the time remaining to maturity and prevailing market interest rates. T-bills are offered at regularly scheduled auction sales by the Treasury in three maturities, 91 days, 182 days and one year. They are sold to the bidders offering the highest prices.

Treasury notes (medium-term instruments bearing interest coupons payable semiannually, with terms of from two to 10 years) are auctioned by yield; that is, they are sold at or close to par or face value to bidders offering the highest yield which, in turn, becomes the coupon interest payable. T-bonds, having maturities of from 10 to 30 years, are auctioned in the same manner as notes. Outstanding T-bonds and T-notes bear a wide range of coupon interest reflecting the fluctuations in interest rates over the years. The prices quoted do not include accrued interest which must be paid to the seller of the bond if the sale does not take place on the day after one of the interest payment dates.

Under Treasury's STRIPS program, an investor can purchase the obligation to pay the principal amount of a T-bond at maturity without the right to receive interest (a zero coupon bond), or can purchase at discount the right to receive one or more of the interest payments due. Over-the-counter Treasury strips quotations are provided by *The Wall Street Journal* and other financial periodicals. Essentially the same rights are available from various bond dealers through the purchase of interests in unitrusts that hold these securities.

Debt obligations are also offered to the public by government agencies, such as the Government National Mortgage Association (GNMA) and Federal National Mortgage Association (FNMA), which offer mortgage-backed securities the payments of principal and interest on which are guaranteed by the Treasury. Similar mortgage-backed pass-through securities without government guarantees are offered by the Federal Home Loan Mortgage Corporation (FMAC).

GNMA securities are purchased mainly by banks, S&L's, mutual funds and financial institutions. While nominally 30-year instruments, they are, as are almost all pass-through instruments, subject to prepayment as the underlying mortgages are paid off, and have terms averaging about 8–12 years.

Treasury and agency issues are non-certificated, that is, the purchaser receives no certificate or other paper evidence of the obligation (other than a confirmation slip from a broker). Instead, transactions are entered into the Federal Reserve Board's book entry system and recorded electronically. Contributing to the prices (or yields) of Treasury obligations, aside from the absence of a risk premium, is the exemption of interest from state and local taxes; likewise, interest on state and municipal obligations is exempt from federal tax (and, generally, income tax of the state of issue).

Options, futures and futures options are offered on all Treasury securities on domestic (and some foreign) exchanges. Delivery under the options and futures contracts is to be made of the type of security to which the contract relates with a specified period to maturity.

T-BILL FUTURES AND OPTIONS

T-bill quotations are in terms of yields. They show the bid and asked yields for various maturity dates computed on a discount basis, and the bond equivalent yield based on asked prices.

In *The Wall Street Journal* of September 28, 1989, for example, the quote for T-bills maturing on February 22, 1990 were: bid - 7.85; asked - 7.81 and (bond equivalent) based on asked prices 8.18.

The discount yield of a T-bill is computed as:

Yield = [(Face Value − Price) × 360/days to maturity]/Face Value. Assume, the price for a six month bill is 942 ($9,420 for a bill paying $10,000 at maturity in 182 days) the discount yield is (58 × 360) = 20,880/182 = 114.73/1000 = 11.47%.

The "bond equivalent yield" is based on a 365-day year and the price paid. The formula is:

[(Face Value − Price) × 365/days to maturity]/by the Price. In this case, using the same price of 942, it is 12.35%.

A T-bill futures offered on the International Monetary Market (IMM) of the Chicago Mercantile Exchange (CME) (the primary contract market for such futures) call for delivery of bills with 90 days to maturity. Each contract is for $1,000,000 in face value. The short position must deliver to the long $1,000,000 in bills on the delivery date at the futures price specified in the contract. Futures quotations show, in lieu of prices, the open, high, low and settlement "indexes" for each delivery month. The index figure is actually yield expressed as 100 (yield × 100). For instance, if the yield is 8%, the index would be 92. The quotation line then shows the yield normally expressed as a percentage figure based on the settlement index. Contracts mature in March, June, September and December of each year with the most distant contract maturing in two years.

Example 3–2

In quotations on September 26, 1989, the settlement indexes for December, March and June of 1990, were shown as 92.52, 92.67 and 92.70, with corresponding settlement yields of 7.48, 7.33 and 7.30. The futures price, the amount payable by the buyer upon delivery of the T-bills, is derived from the index. Since the yields used in computing the indexes are the discount rather than the bond equivalent yields, the price is determined by applying the formula set forth above. The futures price based on the index of 92.52 is: $1,000,000 [(90 × .0748 × $1,000,000)/360] = $981,300. The holder of a long December position acquired with a futures index of 92.52 is entitled to purchase $1,000,000 in face amount of T-bills maturing in 90 days for this price on the date delivery is called for. If short-term interest rates decrease, the value of the bills may be $990,000, and the contract can be closed out (in the same manner as commodity futures contracts) for a gain of $8,700.

A long T-bill futures position will typically be taken by a person seeking to hedge against a decrease in interest rates, such as a lender who contemplates making a loan in the future or rolling over outstanding loans. Futures positions may also be acquired by speculators seeking to profit from interest rate fluctuations. The futures quotations given above indicate a view that short-term interest rates will decrease.

TREASURY NOTE AND BOND FUTURES

Treasury bond futures are by far the most actively traded interest rate instruments on the exchanges where offered. Futures prices are quoted in terms of the price of a bond bearing an 8% coupon with no less than 15 years to maturity (or the earliest call date) with an average term to maturity of 20 years. Each contract calls for the delivery of bonds with a face value of $100,000. The futures prices are quoted in terms of points and 32d's of par. Thus, a price of 98–25 translates to $98,000 plus 25/32 × $1,000 = 98,781.25. Each point or "tick" equals $31.25. The quoted price reflects a yield (based on the average term to maturity of 20 years) of 8.535%, which figure is included in the published futures quotation. A $100,000 contract requires initial margin of $2,500. The bonds delivered if the contract is not closed out must have at least 15 years of their terms remaining (and not be callable before 15 years). In the case of the contract described above, the contract could be closed out at a gain if yields on T-bonds with maturities of 15–20 years remaining dropped below 8.535%.

While trading in T-note futures does not approach the volume of T-bond futures, T-note futures are traded under basically the same rules, except that the quoted yields are based on contracts calling for delivery of 5-year and 2-year notes.

ENDNOTES

[1] Congress deliberately excluded commodities from the definition of "property" in Section 1233(e)(2)(A).

[2] Section 1256(a).

[3] Section 1256(c).

[4] Section 1256(g)(1).

[5] Section 1256(g).

[6] CEA Section 4a, 7 U.S.C. 6(a) (1982).

[7] Rev. Rul. 86-7, 1986-1 C.B. 295; Rev. Rul. 86-72, 1986-1 C.B. 286.

[8] Rev. Rul. 87-43, 1987-1 C.B. 252.

[9] Section 988(c)(1)(B)(iii).

[10] Section 988(a)(1)(A).

[11] Section 988(c)(1)(D)(ii).

[12] Section 988(c)(1)(D)(i).

[13] Section 988(a)(1)(A).

[14] Section 1256(e)(1); Section 1256(e)(2)(C)

CHAPTER 4

INTEREST RATE SWAPS

OBJECTIVE

After completing this chapter you will understand:

- How and why swaps were created.
- The basic economic and financial effects of swaps.
- How swaps are used to control risk.
- The tax effects of the payments by parties and counterparties.

INTRODUCTION

The discussion in this section assumes that transactions do not come within the purview of Section 1259, which was added by the 1997 Tax Relief Act. That section, which affects short sales and certain other transactions, requires taxpayers to recognize gain (but not loss) on entering into a constructive sale of any appreciated position in stock, partnership interests, or certain debt instruments. If Section 1259 applies, gain is recognized as if the position were sold or terminated at its fair market value on the date of the constructive sale. Section 1259 applies to any constructive sale after June 8, 1997. A "constructive sale" for purposes of Section 1259 includes:

- A short sale of the same or substantially identical property,
- An "offsetting" notional principal contract with respect to the same or substantially identical property,
- A futures or forward contract to deliver the same or substantially identical property, or
- Other transactions having the same effect as the above transactions.

The interest rate swap market was created due to arbitrage (price discrepancy) opportunities in the fixed versus floating interest rate markets. Interest rates are extremely volatile. Investors who purchase fixed rate obligations assume the risk that interest rates will change. Therefore, investors will require a premium, usually in the form of an increased interest rate, before purchasing fixed rate obligations. The premium when interest rates are low is often higher than the premium when interest rates are high. When interest rates are high, investors are willing to lock in these high rates while receiving only a small premium for assuming the risk that interest rates will rise further. This creates an arbitrage. It is this arbitrage that financial institutions intended to capture resulting in interest rate swap agreements.

During the early eighties, corporations issuing bonds with a fixed rate of interest realized that investors required too great a premium for assuming the risk that interest rates would change. The cost to a corporation of issuing fixed rate debt combined with an interest swap from a bank or brokerage firm was cheaper than issuing straight floating rate debt.

The swap market has virtually exploded since the early eighties. The swap market has made it possible for corporations and financial institutions to create securities that will solve any issuer's problem. Common variations on the general theme of interest rate swaps are: caps, collars, callable swaps, and swaptions. These products will be discussed later on in the chapter.

INTEREST RATE SWAPS

An interest rate swap is an agreement between a party and a counterparty, which provides that each one will make payments to the other of amounts equal to the interest accruing on a hypothetical debt ("the notional principal"). One of the parties will usually make payments based on a floating or adjustable rate tied to an interest rate index, usually the London Interbank Offered Rate ("LIBOR"). LIBOR is the average rate offered by five major London area banks for Eurodollar deposits for terms of from three months to one year. The counterparty will make payments based on a fixed annual percentage rate.

In the "plain vanilla" interest rate swap, payments are usually due on the same dates and are offset, i.e., one of the parties makes a net payment to the other. The typical situation usually involves one party who has or intends to issue a debt instrument providing for a fixed rate of interest. The party has investments whose rate of return fluctuates with changes in the interest rate. The party wants the rate of interest paid on their debt instrument to approximate the rate earned on their investments. Therefore, the party wishes to tie the interest rate paid on their debt instrument to an interest rate index. A swap dealer will offer an interest rate swap which will match the interest rate and terms desired, taking a number of basis points as his commission. The fixed rate to be paid is, in effect, changed to a floating rate.

Dealer Network

Swap agreements initially provided that the rights and obligations of either party could not be assigned to another person without the consent of the counterparty, i.e., swaps were not negotiable or tradable.

Interest rate swaps are similar to forward contracts. Interest rate swaps are privately negotiated between the parties without the intermediation of an exchange. The interest rates involved depend, as in the case of debt instruments, on market rates and the creditworthiness of the respective parties.

During the late eighties, a network of swap dealers consisting of about 150 banks and financial institutions worldwide developed. This network of dealers developed a standardized swap contract which details the rights and obligations of the parties. The dealer network also provides quotes on swaps acting somewhat similar to an exchange. The dealers in the network act as intermediaries guaranteeing the obligations of the parties entering into swaps with the dealer. The dealer network allows swap positions to be transferred, terminated or otherwise liquidated.

For more information on the economics of interest rate swaps, the author suggests *Practicing Law Institute Handbook for 1989*, "Interest Rate and Currency Swaps 1989," which contains a concise explanation of the economic and technical aspects of interest rate swaps.

Economics

Swaps can be a very valuable management tool for the party with long-term liabilities and rolled over short-term assets. A swap permits a party that can borrow at low rates to, in effect, sell this advantage to a party unable to access the market on such favorable terms, and to permit the party with the lower credit rating to borrow funds at a lower effective fixed rate than would otherwise be available. The swap serves to alter the party's all-in costs of borrowing and permits the party to substitute exposure to the risks of fixed rate borrowing to those of a floating rate (and vice versa) that may more closely match the character of its cash flows. Consider two very different corporations:

Example 4–1

DBL Corporation is fiscally sound with a highly structured balance sheet which is rated AAA by Standard & Poors and Aaa by Moody's. DBL is able to borrow at a long-term fixed rate of 8%. However, many of its investments and other financial assets yield a floating rate return. DBL can borrow funds at LIBOR without having to pay a premium due to its highly rated balance sheet.

Example 4–2

DLS Corporation is not as financially sound as DBL Corporation. Its balance sheet is less secure and therefore not as highly rated. DLS Corporation will have to pay a 10% fixed rate for long-term funds. If DLS Corporation issues floating debt, it will have to pay LIBOR plus 1 percentage point.

The typical non-intermediated interest rate swap arrangement would be as follows:

> DBL issues long-term fixed rate debt at 8% and then enters into an interest rate swap with DLS under which it receives a fixed rate of 8.5%.

> DLS issues floating rate debt at LIBOR plus 1 and receives LIBOR flat under its swap with DBL.

The result is that DLS's total fixed borrowing cost is reduced from 10% to 9.5% (the fixed rate of 8.5% plus a 1% premium on the floating debt). This represents a savings to DLS of 500 basis points. DBL, on the other hand, pays a floating rate equal to LIBOR on its swap with DLS and receives a profit of 500 basis points on the fixed rate paid under its interest rate swap with DLS.

The interest rate swap allows DBL to match cash flows from its financial asset portfolio with its outstanding debt. Since DBL's income from financial assets is based on floating rates, DBL was able to substitute a floating rate for a fixed rate on the debt it has issued.

As interest rates change, an interest rate swap can become a valuable asset which can be assigned to the counterparty or a third party for value. It may also become a liability if interest rates move against the holder of the position which the holder will be willing to pay another party to assume. In this regard, interest rate swaps are similar to options or forwards. Depending on whether interest rates rise or fall, interest rate swaps may be profitable (in-the-money) or unprofitable (out-of-the-money).

Consider DBL Corporation, the corporation in the previous example. If LIBOR should increase to 10.5%, then DBL's LIBOR swap position would be out-of-the-money (unprofitable). DBL had agreed to pay to DLS a floating rate equal to LIBOR and to receive from DLS 8.5% fixed. Assuming the parties have the right to offset, DBL is required to pay net to DLS 2.0%.

DBL may be willing to negotiate with a third party or a swap dealer to assume its rights and obligations under its floating rate position with DLS. Assuming DBL chooses to negotiate with a swap dealer, the dealer could either agree to negotiate with DLS to terminate the swap or find another counterparty to agree to a LIBOR versus 8.5% fixed rate swap position in exchange for a premium paid by the dealer. The premium will approximate DBL's continuing obligation to pay net 2% for the term of the interest rate swap. Of course, since DBL entered into the interest rate swap to match cash flows from its financial asset portfolio with its outstanding debt, DBL should be receiving higher returns from its asset portfolio. DBL has also received a benefit in that the long-term fixed rate debt at 8% is below the current rate. If DBL were to issue fixed rate debt today, it would have to issue debt at a rate in excess of 10.5%.

DLS's position on the other hand is in-the-money. DLS might be willing to assign its swap position in exchange for a premium, leaving it free to enter into a new swap. DLS continues to be liable on its floating rate debt at LIBOR plus 1 which it previously issued, i.e., 11.5%.

In the case of standardized dealer intermediated swaps, the dealer will, in effect, find an assignee. In some instances, a swap party may desire to unbundle the position and assign only one of the legs (usually the obligation leg). This can also be arranged by a dealer. One of the benefits of a dealer intermediated swap is that because swap terms generally require consent of the counterparty for any assignment, where the dealer is the counterparty, consent is not a problem. In this respect, the swap resembles a forward contract since the rights and obligations under the swap can be terminated by assignment, cancellation or entering into an offsetting contract. The right to receive a stream of fixed interest rate payments is very liquid, and its sale would not appear to require the consent of the obligor, because the seller's obligation to make payments to the counterparty is not affected.

INCOME TAX TREATMENT

Income Tax Summary

The principal tax problems arising from interest rate swaps involve the timing and character of income and deductions. The IRS has issued regulations[1] which address the issue of timing and also provide guidance regarding the character of income and deductions from interest rate swap agreements.

The regulations deal with notional principal contracts in general. The regulations apply to interest rate, currency, basis, commodity, equity and equity base, caps and floors. The discussion below will be limited to the tax rules affecting interest rate swaps. The regulations define a notional principal contract as a financial instrument which provides for payments of amounts by one party to another, at specified intervals, calculated by reference to a specific index upon a notional principal amount, in exchange for a specified consideration or a promise to pay similar amounts.[2]

A specific index is defined as:

1. A fixed rate, price or amount;

2. A series of fixed rates or amounts (including stepped rate swaps);

3. An objective index (one which is based on objective financial information not within the control of the parties, e.g., a broad based equity index); or

4. An interest rate regularly used in normal lending transactions between unrelated persons.[3]

Excluded from the definition are:

1. Section 1256 contracts, futures, forwards and options; and

2. Options to enter into swaps.

Most interest rate swaps are positions in actively traded personal property and therefore subject to the loss deferral provisions of the straddle rules (see Chapter 6).

The regulations separate payments made or received into three categories:

1. Periodic payments;[3]

2. Nonperiodic payments;[4] and

3. Termination payments.[5]

The regulations provide that the net income or deductions from an interest rates swap are included in or deducted from gross income in the taxable year. Net income or expense is the sum of all periodic and nonperiodic payments in the taxable year.[6] Termination payments are treated as gain or loss in the taxable year in which the termination took place.[7]

Periodic payments are those payments payable at fixed intervals of one year or less during the term of the swap. All payments are netted annually, and the net amount is to be recognized under the accrual method of accounting. The ratable daily amount of the net amount of all recognized and unrecognized periodic payments are included in or deducted from ordinary income in the taxable year to which they relate.[8]

Certain interest rate swaps have interest rates that vary, or are set in arrears, i.e., the rate is based on an index rate set the following year. If the payment is based on an index rate that varies, or is set in arrears, taxpayers must use the index rate at the close of the current taxable year to determine the net amount.[9] Essentially, the taxpayer takes a snapshot of the rate at year end and uses that rate to approximate the results of the swap. If the taxpayer determines that the rate at the close of the current taxable year does not provide a reasonable estimate of the rate that will apply when the payment is fixed, the taxpayer may use a rate that is reasonable provided that the rate is used consistently from year to year, and the taxpayer uses the same estimate for the purpose of all reports to shareholders and creditors.[10] Any difference between the amount that is recognized under the snapshot approach and the amount which would have been recognized had the actual rate been known is treated as an adjustment to the net income or deduction for the taxable year in which the rate is fixed.[11]

Nonperiodic swap payments are payments that are not periodic payments or termination payments.[12] Generally, there are two types:

1. Nonperiodic swap payments:
   a. Payments not reflecting a market rate of interest;
   b. A prepayment of one leg of a swap; or
   c. The premium for an option to enter into a swap in the taxable year in which the option is exercised.

2. Nonperiodic cap and floor payments, the premium paid or received to enter into a cap or floor agreement.

Nonperiodic payments must be recognized over the term of the interest rate swap in a manner that reflects the economic substance of the swap. Essentially, nonperiodic swap payments are valued using models that are used to price the cap or floor. Most of these models price caps and floors as a series of cash-settlement option contracts. The nonperiodic payment is then allocated among the payment periods based on the relative values of the deemed cash settled option contracts.[13] The allocation must be based on an economic accrual of the nonperiodic payment, i.e., the payments cannot be spread ratably over the period. If the term of the instrument is subject to extension or early termination, the amortizable amounts must be allocated over the reasonable expected term of the instrument.[14]

Up-front payments may be amortized by assuming that the up-front payment represented the present value of a series of equal additional payments made throughout the term of the swap. The discount rate used to calculate those level payments must be the rate used by the parties to determine the amount of the nonperiodic payment. If the rate is not readily ascertainable, the discount rate must be a reasonable rate. The deemed equal payments are then divided into principal and time value components. The sum of the principal payments so determined should equal the nonperiodic payment which is allocated to the applicable period.[15]

Options and forwards to enter into swaps are taxed as either options or forwards unless the taxpayer enters into the swap. Then, the premiums paid for the option or forward are treated as a nonperiodic payment.

Termination payments are payments made or received to extinguish or assign all or part of the rights and obligations of a swap.[16] The termination payments include payments to:

1. Extinguish the swap;

2. Assign the swap to a third party;

3. Exchange the swap for another; or

4. Another payment which has the economic effect of terminating the parties' obligations under the swap.[17]

A termination payment made or received for assigning or terminating one leg of the swap is not a termination payment.[18] A termination payment is recognized in the year the swap is extinguished, assigned or exchanged.[19] At that time, the remaining unamortized nonperiodic payments are also recognized.[20] Termination payments are capital gain or loss; unamortized nonperiodic payments are ordinary.

A termination payment made or received by an assignee is considered a nonperiodic payment and is amortized accordingly.

ENDNOTES

1 Reg. Sec. 1-446-3.

2 Reg. Sec. 1-446-3(c).

3 Reg. Sec. 1-446-3(e).

4 Reg. Sec. 1-446-3(f).

5 Reg. Sec. 1-446-3(h).

6 Reg. Sec. 1-446-3(d).

7 Reg. Sec. 1-446-3(e)(2)(ii).

8 Reg. Sec. 1-446-3(d) and (h).

9 Reg. Sec. 1-446-3(e)(2)(ii) and (iii).

10 Reg. Sec. 1-446-3(e)(2)(ii)

11 Id.

12 Reg. Sec. 1-446-3(f)(1).

13 Reg. Sec. 1-446-3(f)(2).

14 Reg. Sec. 1-446-3(f).

15 Reg. Sec. 1-446-3(f)(2)(iii)(A).

16 Reg. Sec. 1-446-3(h).

17 Reg. Sec. 1-446-3(h)(4)(ii).

18 Reg. Sec. 1-446-3(h)(4)(i).

19 Reg. Sec. 1-446-3(h)(4).

20 Reg. Sec. 1-446-3(h)(2).

CHAPTER 5

CONTINGENT DEBT INSTRUMENTS

OBJECTIVE

After completing this chapter you will understand:

- The basic tax principles relating to contingent debt instruments.

INTRODUCTION

The discussion in this section assumes that transactions do not come within the purview of Section 1259, which was added by the 1997 Tax Relief Act. That section, which affects short sales and certain other transactions, requires taxpayers to recognize gain (but not loss) on entering into a constructive sale of any appreciated position in stock, partnership interests, or certain debt instruments. If Section 1259 applies, gain is recognized as if the position were sold or terminated at its fair market value on the date of the constructive sale. Section 1259 applies to any constructive sale after June 8, 1997. A "constructive sale" for purposes of Section 1259 includes:

- A short sale of the same or substantially identical property,

- An "offsetting" notional principal contract with respect to the same or substantially identical property,

- A futures or forward contract to deliver the same or substantially identical property, or

- Other transactions having the same effect as the above transactions.

Corporations employing innovative financing techniques have issued contingent debt instruments as a way of combining the various restrictions, rights, and contingencies which offset the risks they encounter in the credit markets in which they do business. As corporations have ventured into many of the new international marketplaces, the credit markets, associated with doing business in these international markets, also need to be managed. Contingent debt instruments are a way to manage these risks.

Many of these financial instruments do not fit easily into any of the categories formulated by the tax laws and the treatment of some still remains unclear. Given the complexities of the problems involved, the IRS, Treasury, and Congress have tried to issue regulations which intend to tax contingent debt instruments consistent with the economic consequences attaching to these transactions.

CONTINGENT PAYMENT OBLIGATIONS

The IRS has been struggling with the taxation of contingent payment obligations since 1986. The IRS has received numerous comments on the proposed regulations originally issued in 1986 and even more comments when the proposed regulations were revised in 1991. In February 1994, the IRS issued final OID regulations;[1] however, they did not finalize Reg. Sec. 1.1275-4, containing the rules for contingent payment obligations. On December 16, 1994, the IRS once again issued proposed regulations, in response to the voluminous comments it has received since 1991 when the proposed regulations were revised. The reader should remember that, once again, these rules as they are issued in proposed form will be the subject of numerous comments and a public hearing. Therefore, some adjustment to the rules can be expected, although the changes should be small.

As we have mentioned above, many derivative products are the result of the issuer trying to hedge its interest, currency and credit risks as economically as possible combined with gaining the best tax result possible. These new regulations will be critical to the development of new derivative financial products therefore, we have outlined them below.

The proposed regulations are applicable instruments with one or more non-remote contingent payment, with the exception of the following:

1. Debt instruments that have an issue price determined under IRC. Sec. 1273(b)(4);

2. Variable rate debt instruments;

3. Debt instruments that provide for an alternative payment schedule;

4. REMIC interests and certain other debt instruments that are subject to prepayment;

5. Debt instruments which provide for payments in or with reference to a foreign currency.[2]

One interesting note is that the proposed regulations do not define a contingent payment, other than to say that it is a payment that is not remote. That is, the likelihood that it will occur or will not occur is not remote.[3]

If the contingent debt instrument is issued for money or publicly traded property, the "noncontingent bond method" is used to determine the interest which accrues on the instrument.[4] Under the noncontingent bond method, interest is accrued whether or not the amount of any payment is fixed or determinable in the taxable year. The amount of interest is determined by constructing a projected payment schedule for the debt instrument and accruing interest based on that schedule.[5] This is very similar to the OID rules discussed above. Prior to these proposed regulations, contingencies were generally taxed under a "wait and see" method. The amount of stated interest, if any, was accrued currently, but the contingency remained untaxed until it could be determined. This created all kinds of opportunities to defer interest, and the IRS, in issuing the new contingent debt instrument proposed regulations, is attempting to prevent some of these deferrals.

The projected payment schedule is determined as of the issue date and is based on forward prices, if readily available, or on a projected pattern of expected payments and a projected yield.[6] The following steps describe how the projected payment schedule is determined.

1. First, determine the projected payment schedule.

2. Second, based on the issue price of the debt instrument and the projected payment schedule, determine the projected yield of the debt instrument.

3. Third, determine the daily portions of interest on the debt instrument for the taxable year. This is done by determining the amount of interest which accrues in each accrual period. Essentially, the amount of interest which accrues is the product of the projected yield of the debt instrument and the debt instrument's adjusted issue price at the beginning of the accrual period. Then, dividing the interest accruing in each accrual period into the number of days in the accrual period.

4. Lastly, adjustments must be made for differences between the amount of income or deductions attributable to the debt instrument in a taxable year from projected and actual contingent payments.[7]

The key to the amount of interest which accrues in each accrual period is the projected payment schedule. This schedule, once determined, remains constant throughout the term of the debt instrument.[8] The projected payment schedule is determined by the issuer of the debt instrument.[9]

As discussed above, a contingent payment debt instrument can be viewed as a debt instrument with one or more other financial instruments imbedded therein. The proposed regulations take this approach, by requiring the issuer to price the imbedded instruments to determine the projected payment schedule.[10]

The proposed regulations indicate that the projected payment schedule is determined through the use of quotes for the respective contingencies imbedded in the debt instrument. Where the quote is readily available, the issuer can use any consistent pricing based on bid, ask, or midpoint price quotes.[11] A quote is considered readily available if the contingent payment is substantially similar to a property right, i.e., under reasonably expected market conditions, the value and timing of the amount to be received pursuant to the property right is expected to be substantially the same as the value and timing of the contingent payment.[12]

The proposed regulations recognize that when these instruments are created, the issuer has done so to hedge a determined risk. Further, the instrument was developed to reduce the transaction costs associated with hedging these risks. Therefore, the proposed regulations are requiring the issuer to reprice the components of the debt instrument, by reference to the options, futures or forwards existing in the market to determine a payment schedule under which the instrument can be taxed. This approach works very well when quotes are available in the market place; however, many of these contingent payment instruments were issued simply because the issuer could not find an instrument to adequately hedge their risks. Most corporations issued contingent payment debt instruments because these instruments passed the hedging risk on to the investor. Specifically, a selling point of these contingent payment debt instruments was that these instruments passed on the hedging risks to the holder at a lower cost than acquiring the necessary hedges in the market, or because the necessary hedges did not exist in the market.

Where the quote is not readily available, the proposed regulations require certain steps to back into a price for the contingent payments by determining an existing yield for the debt instrument and pricing the contingent payments consistent with the determined yield. The proposed regulations require the following steps:

1. First, if any of the imbedded financial instruments is subject to a market quote, that should be determined;

2. Second, the issuer is required to determine the projected yield on the debt instrument by using a reasonable rate that approximates existing market conditions, credit quality, and the terms and conditions of the debt instrument; and

3. Third, the issuer is required to select a projected amount for each contingent payment which is not subject to an existing market quote so that the projected yield reasonably reflects the relative expected value of the nonquotable contingent payment.[13]

Let's consider some examples:

Example 5-1 •

On January 1, 1995, DBL Corporation issues for $1,000,000 a debt instrument that matures on December 31, 1999. The instrument has a $1,000,000 stated redemption value payable at maturity. The instrument also provides for the payment of 10,000 times the increase, if any, in the value of the S & P 500 index from January 1, 1995 to the maturity date.

The right to the contingent payment is substantially similar to a long call option on the S & P 500 index that is exercisable on December 31, 1999. Under the proposed regulations, since quotes are readily available for option on the S & P 500 index, the projected amount for the contingent payment is the forward price of a long call option on the S & P 500. If the debt instrument was based on an index for which there was no readily available quote, the contingent payment would be based on the spot price (current price for the option on the issue date) compounded at the applicable Federal rate for the debt instrument from the issue date to the maturity date.

Example 5-2

On January 1, 1995, DBL Corporation issues for $1,000,000 a debt instrument that matures on December 31, 1999. The debt instrument provides for annual payments of interest at the rate of 6 percent and for a payment at maturity equal to $1,000,000 plus the excess, if any, of the price of 1,000 units of a commodity on the maturity date over $350,000, or less the excess, if any, of $350,000 over the price of 1,000 units of the commodity on the maturity date.

This debt instrument is similar to a debt instrument with an imbedded forward contract for the underlying commodity, as the holder can suffer a loss or receive a gain based on whether the value of the commodity increases. The projected payment schedule for the debt instrument consists of 4 annual payments of $60,000 and a projected amount for the contingency payment at maturity. Assume that the forward price quote to purchase the commodity on December 31, 1999 is readily available. If the forward price to purchase 1,000 units of the commodity is $350,000, then the projected amount of the contingency payment is $1,000,000. Unlike the option contract, the forward contract has no premium as the holder has the downside risk as well as the upside profit.

Example 5–2 (continued)

Therefore the contingency relating to the forward contract is zero. Of course, the issuer could discount the cost of the forward contract. If the forward price to purchase 1,000 units of the commodity is $370,000, then the projected amount of the contingency payment is $1,020,000 ($20,000 relating to the forward contract). If the price of the forward contract is not readily available, the issuer will have to determine the projected yield which would include the assumed cost of the forward contract and develop a projected payment schedule accordingly.[14]

The next question to consider is this: what happens to the differences between the projected and the actual contingent payments? If the amount is a net positive adjustment it is considered additional interest in the taxable year that it is realized.[15] If the adjustment is negative, it reduces interest for the taxable year, but not less than zero and any excess is carried over to be offset against future interest income that will accrue based on the projected payment schedule.[16] In the year of sale or other disposition, any negative adjustment is considered to reduce the amount realized of the holder and is considered income from the discharge of indebtedness of the issuer.[17]

Let's consider an example:

Example 5–3

Assume that DBL, a calendar year holder, purchases a debt instrument on July 1, 1995 at original issue for $1,050. The projected payment schedule provides for the following payments:

1. December 31, 1995   — $ 100.

2. December 31, 1996   — $1,100.

Assume that based on the projected payment schedule, DBL's total daily portions of interest would be $50 for 1995 and $100 for 1996. Assume further that on December 31, 1995, the actual contingent payment was $25. Since DBL has no net positive adjustment, DBL would have a net negative adjustment of $75 ($100 projected payment − $25 contingent payment for 1995). DBL would not be required to accrue the $50 interest payment. Further, DBL would carry over the remaining $25 net negative adjustment to 1996.

If the actual contingent payment was $1,150 in 1996, instead of the projected payment of $1,100, then DBL would net the $25 carryforward negative adjustment from 1995 against the $50 net positive adjustment in 1996 and include $25 as interest income in 1996.

If the actual contingent payment was $1,010 in 1996, instead of the projected payment of $1,100, then DBL would have an additional negative adjustment of $90 in 1996. DBL would combine this negative adjustment with the $25 carryforward negative adjustment from 1995. The total net negative adjustment of $115 would reduce to zero the $100 total daily portion of interest for 1996, and the remaining $15 net negative adjustment would reduce the amount realized on the retirement of the debt instrument in 1996.[18]

What is the holder's basis in the debt instrument? What is the adjusted issue price? The projected payments are treated as the actual payments for purposes of making adjustments to issue price and basis and determining the amount of any contingent payment made on a scheduled retirement. This is because the difference between the projected and actual payments is treated as an adjustment to income or deductions.[19]

Therefore, the adjusted issue price is equal to the debt instrument's issue price, increased by the interest previously accrued on the debt instrument without regard to the net positive or negative adjustments, decreased by the amount of any noncontingent payment and the projected amount of any contingent payment previously made on the debt instrument.[20]

A holder's basis in a debt instrument is increased by the interest previously accrued by the holder on the debt instrument determined without regard to any net positive or negative adjustments taken into account, and decreased by the amount of any noncontingent payment and the projected amount of any contingent payment previously made on the debt instrument to the holder.[21]

For purposes of determining the amount realized by a holder and the repurchase price paid by the issuer on the scheduled retirement of a debt instrument, a holder is treated as receiving, and the issuer is treated as paying, the projected amount of any contingent payment at maturity. The amount realized on a scheduled retirement of a debt instrument and the issuer's repurchase price on retirement; however, it may be reduced by the negative carryforwards determined in the taxable year of retirement.[22]

An unscheduled retirement of a debt instrument (or the receipt of a pro-rata prepayment that is treated as a retirement of a portion of a debt instrument) is treated as a sale or exchange of the debt instrument (or pro-rata portion of the debt instrument) by the holder to the issuer for the amount paid by the issuer to the holder.[23]

Let's consider an example:

Example 5–4

Assume the same facts as in Example 5–3 above. The adjusted issue price of the debt instrument and DBL's adjusted basis would be increased by the daily portion of the interest on the debt instrument, i.e., $50 in 1995. The adjusted issue price of the debt instrument and DBL's adjusted basis would be decreased by the projected amount of payment on that date. The adjusted issue price and basis would be computed as follows: add the $50 daily interest accrual, to the $1,050 DBL paid for the debt instrument and subtract $100, the projected amount of the contingent payment. The adjusted issue price and basis on January 1, 1996 is $1,000.

For purposes of retirement, DBL is treated as receiving $1,100 at maturity, the projected amount of the contingent payment on December 31, 1996. DBL's adjusted basis immediately before retirement is $1,100 — $1,000 basis on January 1, 1996 plus $100 contingent interest accrual from the projected payment schedule. DBL would take net positive adjustments into income as interest in 1996. If DBL had a net carryforward adjustment DBL would have a loss on the retirement equal to the net carryforward adjustment.[24]

How about character? Any gain recognized by the holder on a sale or exchange is interest income.[25] Any loss recognized by the holder on a sale or exchange is ordinary loss to the extent of the holder's total interest inclusions on the debt, any additional loss is treated as a loss from the sale or exchange of the debt instrument, taxed consistently with the holder's treatment of the debt instrument as either capital or ordinary.

Let's consider some examples:

Example 5–5

On January 1, 1997, DBL, a calendar year taxpayer, sells a debt instrument for $1,350. On that date DBL has an adjusted basis in the debt instrument of $1,200. DBL also has a negative adjustment carryforward of $50 on January 1, 1997.

The $50 negative adjustment on January 1, 1997 results in a negative adjustment carryforward for 1997, the taxable year of the sale. As a result, DBL realizes a $100 gain on the sale of the debt instrument.

Example 5–6

On January 1, 1996, DBL, a calendar year taxpayer, purchases a debt instrument at original issue for $1,000. The debt instrument is a capital asset in DBL's hands. The debt instrument calls for a payment of $1,000 at maturity in December 2001, and for quotable (readily available) contingent payments on December 31, 1997, 1999 and 2001. The projected payment schedule calls for projected payments of $275 on December 31, 1997, $200 on December 31, 1999, and $1,127 on December 31, 2001. The projected yield on the debt instrument is 10 percent, compounded annually. Based on the projected payment schedule, the total daily portions of interest would be $100 for 1996, $110 for 1997 and $93.50 for 1998.

Assume that the payment made on December 31, 1997 is $150, rather than $275. DBL has a negative adjustment of $125 on the debt instrument for 1997. The negative adjustment reduces to zero the $110 interest DBL would otherwise include in income in 1997. Because DBL had $100 of interest inclusions for 1996, DBL will have an ordinary loss of $15 for 1997.

Assume that DBL sells the debt instrument for $950 on December 31, 1998. DBL has an adjusted basis of $1,028.50 ($1,000 original basis, plus the projected interest inclusions of $100, $110 and $93.50 less the $275 projected contingent payment). As a result, DBL realizes a $78.50 loss on the sale of the debt instrument. Further, because the total amount of DBL's interest inclusions as of December 31, 1998 ($100 in 1996 and $93.50 in 1998) exceeds the total amount of negative adjustments on the debt instrument ($15 in 1997) by more than $78.50, the loss is ordinary.

Example 5–7

Assume the same facts as in Example 5–6 above, except that the payment actually made on December 31, 1997 is $0, rather than $275. DBL has a negative adjustment of $275 on the debt instrument for 1997. The negative adjustment reduces to zero the $110 interest DBL would otherwise include in income in 1997. Because DBL had $100 of interest inclusions for 1996, DBL will have an ordinary loss of $100 for 1997 and a $65 carryforward negative adjustment on January 1, 1998.

Assume that DBL sells the debt instrument for $900 on January 1, 1998. DBL has an adjusted basis of $935 ($1,000 original basis, plus the projected interest inclusions of $100, $110 less the $275 projected contingent payment). Because DBL has no other interest accruals to offset the $65 negative adjustment, the $65 carryforward reduces the amount DBL realizes from the sale of the debt instrument from $900 to $835. As a result, DBL realizes a $100 loss on the sale of the debt instrument. Further, because the total amount of DBL's interest inclusions as of January 1, 1998 do not exceed the total amount of negative adjustments on the debt instrument, the loss is a capital loss. Remember, the facts indicated that the debt instrument was a capital asset in DBL's hands.[26]

In certain circumstances, the holder's basis in the debt instrument will be different than the adjusted issue price, i.e., a subsequent holder that purchases the debt instrument for more or less than the instrument's adjusted issue price. A holder whose basis in the debt instrument is different from the adjusted issue price accrues interest and makes adjustments based on the projected payment schedule which is determined on the issue date.[27] However, upon acquiring the debt instrument, the holder must reasonably allocate any difference between the adjusted issue price and the basis to the daily portions of interest or projected payments over the remaining term of the debt instrument.[28] The general rules for premium and discount do not apply.[29] If a contingent payment instrument is exchange listed property, the holder can amortize the difference over the remaining term of the debt instrument.[30]

If a holder's basis in a debt instrument exceeds the debt instrument's adjusted issue price, the amount allocated to a daily portion of interest or to a projected payment is treated as a negative adjustment on the date the daily portion accrues or the payment is made. The holder's basis is reduced by the amount the holder treats as a negative adjustment.[31]

Alternatively, if a holder's basis in a debt instrument is less than the debt instrument's adjusted issue price, the amount allocated to a daily portion of interest or to a projected payment is treated as a positive adjustment on the date the daily portion accrues or the payment is made. The holder's basis is increased by the amount the holder treats as a positive adjustment.[32]

Let's continue with some examples:

Example 5–8

On July 1, 1997, DBL purchases for $1,405 a debt instrument that matures on December 31, 1998, and promises to pay on the maturity date $1,000 plus the increase, if any, in the price of a specified commodity from the issue date to the maturity date. The debt

Example 5–8 (continued)

instrument was originally issued on January 1, 1996 for an issue price of $1,000. DBL is a calendar year taxpayer. The projected payment schedule for the debt instrument provides for a single payment at maturity of $1,350. Thus the debt instrument has a projected yield of 10.25 percent, compounded semiannually. On July 1, 1997, the debt instrument had an adjusted issue price of $1,162. The increase in the value over its adjusted issue price is due to an increase in the expected amount of the contingent payment (i.e., the value of the underlying commodity increased) and not to a decrease in market interest rates.

DBL's basis in the debt instrument is $1,405. Therefore, DBL will be required to allocate the $243 difference to the contingent payment at maturity, because the increase was due to the increase in the value of the specified commodity and not market interest rates.

Based on the projected payment schedule, $60 of interest accrues from July 1, 1997 to December 31, 1997. This accrual is based on the product of the debt instrument's adjusted issue price and the projected yield for the semiannual period ($1,162 * 10.25 percent / 2). Therefore, DBL's adjusted basis in the debt instrument is $1,465 ($1,405 + $60). Since the $243 is allocated to the contingent payment at maturity, DBL has no negative or positive adjustment for 1997.

Assume that the payment actually made at maturity is $1,400, rather than the projected $1,350. DBL would have a positive adjustment of $50 which would offset the $243 negative adjustment above which was allocated to the contingent payment at maturity. As a result, DBL would have a $193 negative adjustment for 1998. Based on the projected payment schedule, $128 of interest accrues during 1998. Therefore, the $193 negative adjustment would reduce to zero the 1998 interest accrual, leaving a $65 negative adjustment. Because DBL included $60 as a positive adjustment in 1997, $60 of the remaining $65 negative adjustment is an ordinary loss, and the remaining $5 is a loss on the retirement of a debt instrument.[33]

Example 5–9

On January 1, 1998, DBL purchases for $910 a debt instrument that pays semi-annual interest of 7 percent. The debt instrument matures on December 31, 2000, and promises to pay on the maturity date $1,000 plus or minus $10 times the positive or negative difference, if any, between a specified amount and the value of an index on the maturity date. However, the payment on December 31, 2000, may not be less than $650. The debt instrument was originally issued on January 1, 1996 for an issue price of $1,000. DBL is a calendar year taxpayer. The projected payment schedule for the debt instrument provides for semiannual payments of $35 and a payment at maturity of $1,175. On January 1, 1998, the debt instrument had an adjusted issue price of $1,160. Since the time the debt instrument was issued market rates of interest have increased from 10 percent to 13 percent. In addition, because of a decrease in the relevant index, the expected contingent payment has decreased by approximately 9 percent.

Example 5–9 (continued)

DBL's basis in the debt instrument is $910. Therefore, DBL will be required to allocate the $150 difference to daily portions of interest or projected payments. This amount will be a positive adjustment taken into account at the time of the interest accrual or the projected payment is made.

Based on the forward prices on January 1, 1998, DBL determines that approximately $105 of the difference relates to the contingent payment. DBL will allocate the remaining $45 to the daily interest accruals.[34]

Example 5–10

Assume the same facts as in Example 5–9 above except that DBL allocates $49 to daily interest accrual and $101 to the contingent payment. In 1998, DBL has a total of $104.68 of daily portions of interest, receives two semiannual $35 payments and has a $13.32 positive adjustment from the allocation. Thus, DBL has $118 of interest income from the debt instrument for 1998 ($104.68 of interest and 13.32 net positive adjustment). On December 31, 1998 DBL has a $958 adjusted basis ($910 original basis, plus $104.68 of interest, plus $13.32 of net positive adjustment, less $70 of interest payments). If DBL sells the debt instrument on December 31, 1998 for $950, DBL would have a $8 ordinary loss.[35]

What about hedges? In general, the proposed regulations provide for the integration of a qualifying debt instrument with a hedge or combination of hedges if the combined cash flows of the components are substantially equivalent to the cash flows on a fixed or variable rate debt instrument. The proposed regulations also provide their own integration rules and therefore, a separate accounting is not required of each component.[36] A qualifying debt instrument is any contingent payment debt instrument other than a tax-exempt obligation.[37]

A hedge is any financial instrument such that the combined cash flows of the financial instrument and the qualifying debt instrument permit the calculation of a yield to maturity. A financial instrument that hedges currency risk is not a contingent instrument hedge.[38] A taxpayer cannot treat a debt instrument it issues as a hedge of a debt instrument it holds and a debt instrument it holds cannot be a hedge of a debt instrument it issues.[39]

The definition of a financial instrument is fairly broad and includes a spot, forward, or futures contracts, an option, a notional principal contract, a debt instrument, or a similar instrument or combination or series of financial instruments, but not stock.[40]

As with all IRS regulations, specific rules are required to be satisfied before taxpayers can avail themselves of the integration section. Namely:

1. The taxpayer must identify the transaction on or before the date the taxpayer enters into the hedge;

2. None of the parties can be related;

3. Both the qualifying debt instrument and the hedge must be entered into by the same person;

4. If a foreign person issues or acquires a qualifying debt instrument, all income associated with the debt instrument must be effectively connected with the foreign person's U.S. trade or business, throughout the term of the instrument;

5. The qualifying debt instrument, any other debt that is part of the same issue as the qualifying debt instrument, or the hedge cannot be part of an integrated transaction which has been terminated ("legged-out"), and

6. The hedge is entered into on or after the date the qualifying debt instrument is issued or acquired.[41]

The above rules contain a section on legging-in and legging-out. The leg-in date is the date that the taxpayer identifies the debt instrument as part of an integrated transaction. Legging-out is when the taxpayer disposes of or otherwise terminates the integrated transaction. If the taxpayer disposes of both legs of the integrated transaction on the same day he is considered to have sold or otherwise disposed of the synthetic debt instrument at its fair market value on the leg-out date and income, deduction, gain or loss is realized and recognized on the leg-out date. Additionally, appropriate adjustments are made as of the leg-out date to reflect any difference between the fair market value of the qualifying debt instrument and the adjusted issue price of the qualifying debt instrument.[42]

SUMMARY

Investors should remember that the IRS has been struggling with the taxation of contingent payment obligations since 1986. This latest attempt by the IRS represents a major step in recognizing that investors expect the taxation of contingent debt instruments to approximate their economics. These latest regulations are in response to the voluminous comments that the IRS has received since 1991. The reader should also remember that these rules are issued in proposed form and will be the subject of additional comments and a public hearing. Therefore, some adjustment to the rules can be expected.

ENDNOTES

1 See, Federal Register, 59 FR 4799.

2 Prop. Reg. Sec. 1.12754(a)(2).

3 Prop. Reg. Sec. 1.12754(a)(5).

4 Prop. Reg. Sec. 1.12754(b)(1).

5 Prop. Reg. Sec. 1.12754(b)(2).

6 Id.

7 Prop. Reg. Sec. 1.12754(b)(3).

8 Prop. Reg. Sec. 1.12754(b)(4).

9 Prop. Reg. Sec. 1.12754(b)(4)(iv).

[10] Prop. Reg. Sec. 1.1275-4(b)(4).

[11] Prop. Reg. Sec. 1.1275-4(b)(4)(i)(E).

[12] Prop. Reg. Sec. 1.1275-4(b)(4)(i)(C).

[13] Prop. Reg. Sec. 1.1275-4(b)(4)(ii).

[14] Prop. Reg. Sec. 1.1275-4(b)(4)(vi).

[15] Prop. Reg. Sec. 1.1275-4(b)(6)(ii).

[16] Prop. Reg. Sec. 1.1275-4(b)(6)(iii).

[17] Prop. Reg. Sec. 1.1275-4(b)(6)(iii)(C)(2).

[18] Prop. Reg. Sec. 1.1275-4(b)(6)(v).

[19] Prop. Reg. Sec. 1.1275-4(b)(7).

[20] Prop. Reg. Sec. 1.1275-4(b)(7)(ii).

[21] Prop. Reg. Sec. 1.1275-4(b)(7)(iii).

[22] Prop. Reg. Sec. 1.1275-4(b)(7)(iv).

[23] Prop. Reg. Sec. 1.1275-4(b)(7)(v).

[24] Prop. Reg. Sec. 1.1275-4(b)(7)(vi).

[25] Prop. Reg. Sec. 1.1275-4(b)(8).

[26] Prop. Reg. Sec. 1.1275-4(b)(8)(v).

[27] Prop. Reg. Sec. 1.1275-4(b)(9)(i)(A).

[28] Id.

[29] Prop. Reg. Sec. 1.1275-4(b)(9)(i)(D).

[30] Prop. Reg. Sec. 1.1275-4(b)(9)(i)(E).

[31] Prop. Reg. Sec. 1.1275-4(b)(9)(i)(B).

[32] Prop. Reg. Sec. 1.1275-4(b)(9)(i)(C).

[33] Prop. Reg. Sec. 1.1275-4(b)(9)(i)(F).

[34] Id.

[35] Id.

[36] Prop. Reg. Sec. 1.1275-6(a).

[37] Prop. Reg. Sec. 1.1275-6(b)(1).

[38] Prop. Reg. Sec. 1.1275-6(b)(2)(i).

[39] Prop. Reg. Sec. 1.1275-6(b)(2)(ii).

[40] Prop. Reg. Sec. 1.1275-6(b)(3).

[41] Prop. Reg. Sec. 1.1275-6(c).

[42] Prop. Reg. Sec. 1.1275-6(d).

CHAPTER 6

STRADDLES

OBJECTIVE

After reading this chapter you should know:

- The definition of a straddle as that term is used in the market.

- The basic economics of straddles.

- How and why straddles are used in the stock market.

- What types of financial instruments are used.

- The definition of a straddle as that term is used in Section 1092 of the Internal Revenue Code.

- The basic tax concepts surrounding the use of straddles.

INTRODUCTION

The discussion in this section assumes that transactions do not come within the purview of Section 1259, which was added by the 1997 Tax Relief Act. That section, which affects short sales and certain other transactions, requires taxpayers to recognize gain (but not loss) on entering into a constructive sale of any appreciated position in stock, partnership interests, or certain debt instruments. If Section 1259 applies, gain is recognized as if the position were sold or terminated at its fair market value on the date of the constructive sale. Section 1259 applies to any constructive sale after June 8, 1997. A "constructive sale" for purposes of Section 1259 includes:

- A short sale of the same or substantially identical property,

- An "offsetting" notional principal contract with respect to the same or substantially identical property,

- A futures or forward contract to deliver the same or substantially identical property, or

- Other transactions having the same effect as the above transactions.

This chapter will provide basic definitions of what a straddle is, how it is used in the market and attempt to outline some of the basic tax principles regarding straddles. Much of the tax law regarding straddles revolves around the government's attempt to prevent abusive practices by speculators, securities dealers and their clients to defer taxes on income, convert capital loss into ordinary or age holding periods to benefit from the reduced long-term capital gains rates, or benefit from the dividend received deduction. As the law has developed, Congress has continued to include more and more transactions within the straddle rules. As investors have become increasingly creative, the government has sought to prevent what they believe is an abuse of the rules through broad sweeping Internal Revenue Code provisions. Different anti-abuse rules are contained in various sections of the Internal Revenue Code and the investor is required to review each transaction with an eye toward anticipating what possible abuse the government was trying to protect against.

The tax straddle rules are contained in IRC Section 1092 and the related regulations. However, corporate investors concerned about the dividend received deduction should also review IRC Section 246 concerning when the holding period will be tolled for purposes of the dividends received deduction.

MARKET DEFINITION OF A STRADDLE

A straddle, as that term is used in the market, is generally the holding of two or more positions that exactly offset each other.

A straddle can be broadly defined as:

1. Two or more offsetting positions which are valued by some type of market which can may be liquidated at any time; and

2. Market forces resulting in a change in value of one position will almost always result in an inverse change in value of the offsetting position, although not necessarily in the same (or even nearly the same) amount.

Straddles are entered into for a wide variety of reasons usually not related to deriving a tax benefit from the transaction. Straddles are used by traders and investors with widely varying willingness to accept exposure to risk in attempting to profit from market changes. Investors will generally enter into a straddle to ensure against market fluctuations. Straddles, may involve complex patterns of long and short positions, may range from the extremely conservative to the very risky, usually with commensurate potential rewards.

Examples of situations where a straddle may be used:

1. An investor may wish to lock in all or a portion of unrealized gain from an appreciated position, or she may wish to protect against any drop in value below a given point. For instance, assume stock X has increased from $10 per share to $15 per share and investor A wishes to guarantee the gain. Investor A may purchase a put option allowing Investor A to sell the stock at $15 per share, or write a call option receiving a premium which will offset (to the extent of the premium) any decrease in the value of X stock, if the shares of X decrease.

2. A corporate money manager or financial institution may wish to minimize risks from adverse fluctuations in foreign exchange and interest rates on financial assets held or to be acquired and/or liabilities incurred or to be incurred. The money manager may enter into a currency swap to shelter both risks, or enter into a forward contract to shelter the currency risk and purchase an interest rate future to shelter the interest rate risk.

3. Corporations whose profits can be adversely affected by commodity prices (for example: growers, processors, or manufacturers) have a need to use straddles to protect their profits against commodity price fluctuations. Many if not all such corporations

actively trade the commodity they produce to reduce the risks associated with fluctuations in commodity prices.

The above definition should not be confused with the Internal Revenue Code Section 1092 definition, which refers to the holding of *offsetting positions in actively traded personal property*.

Congress is aware that straddle transactions play an important non-tax oriented role in many business operations. Therefore, Congress attempted to structure the rules to permit taxpayers to enter into such nontax oriented straddles without adverse tax consequences. The Internal Revenue Code definitions are very specific, and failure to meet one of the definitions could result in negative tax consequences. Additionally, adverse tax consequences may result from faulty tax planning with respect to nontax motivated transactions entered into by taxpayers who lack thorough familiarity with these rules. These definitions will be discussed later on in the chapter.

INTERNAL REVENUE CODE DEFINITION OF A STRADDLE

A straddle is defined in Section 1092(c)(1) as *offsetting positions with respect to personal property*. As with many sections of the Internal Revenue Code, the initial definition is very broad and uses terms which are defined in subsequent paragraphs in the section. Investors who are considering entering into a straddle transaction should be intimately familiar with the Section 1092 definitions. Let's look at the specifics of the definition and break it down to see what transactions it actually covers.

A *position* is defined in Section 1092(d)(2) as an interest (including a futures or forward contract or option) in personal property. A position includes *any* right, obligation or interest with respect to personal property, including ownership of such property, or an option to acquire any of the above as well as any binding contract to purchase or sell actively traded property. The general intent of Section 1092 is to include within the definition of a straddle any transactions where the investor has limited his risk through an offsetting position. Therefore, the definition of a position for purposes of this section is intended to be inclusive.

Personal property is described as any personal property which is actively traded. Actively traded personal property includes any personal property traded on an established financial market, which according to the definition, includes personal property traded on:

1. A national securities exchange;

2. An interdealer quotation system sponsored by a national securities association;

3. A domestic board of trade designated as a contract market by the Commodities Futures Trading Association;

4. A foreign securities exchange or board of trade with analogous regulatory requirements;

5. An interbank market;

6. An interdealer market that provides a reasonable basis for determining fair market value by disseminating recent price quotations or actual prices of recent transactions; or

7. A debt market where recent price quotations for the instrument are readily available from brokers, dealers, or traders.

The intent of item 6 above is to include certain notional principal contracts within the definition of actively traded personal property. Specifically, Regs. Secs. 1.1092(d)1(c)(1) and (2) provide that notional principal contracts will be included in the definition of actively traded property if:

1. Contracts based on the same or substantially similar specified indices are purchased, sold, or entered into on an established financial market; and

2. The rights and obligations of a party to notional principal contract are rights and obligations with respect to personal property and constitute an interest in personal property.

Since Section 1092 is intended to sweep up many of the other transactions which would otherwise escape, the actively traded definition under Section 1092 is intended to cover financial instruments that are liquid or easily offset, even when such instruments are not traded on an exchange or in a recognized secondary market (i.e., swaps). Because many notional principal contracts have a system through which prices are disseminated in the form of recent quotations of financial institutions or in the form of actual prices of recent transactions, a notional principal contract may be considered part of a straddle. Therefore, a debt instrument and a swap, or other notional principal contract that hedges, it can make up a straddle if both are actively traded. If this were not the case, investors would be able to create effective straddles through the use of a combination of any debt instrument and the host of synthetic securities developed by financial institutions. Under Section 1092, a debt instrument is considered personal property in the hands of the investor who holds it.

What about the obligor? If the obligor of a debt instrument hedges his position with a notional principal contract, even though the obligor does not hold property (cash is not property if it is an obligation to repay funds in the issuer's functional currency), Section 1092(d)(7)(A) expressly provides that the obligor's interest in a nonfunctional currency denominated debt obligation is treated as a position in the nonfunctional currency, i.e., property. The notional principal contract is not treated as a debt instrument, since it has neither an issue price nor a stated principal amount. The same rules apply to an obligor; namely, an offsetting swap can create a straddle.

As if this is not enough to avoid these Code provisions forever, Section 1092(d)(3)(A) provides that personal property does not include stock. However, it does include an option to buy or sell stock. For this reason, the holding of an executory contract to purchase actively traded stock and a put option on the same stock will be considered a straddle.

We said that stock is generally not considered personal property, except in some circumstances. Stock will be considered personal property where it is part of a straddle and at least one of the offsetting positions is:

1. An *option* on such stock or on substantially identical stock or securities; or

2. A *position with respect to substantially similar or related property* other than stock as described in Section 1092(d)(3)(B).

For purposes of the above definition, a short sale against the box should *not* be considered a straddle, unless the short sale is in the form of a put option. Also, stock index futures and options *will be* considered a position with respect to substantially similar or related property. Under Regs. Sec. 1.1092(b)4T(b)(3) a stock index is considered to be property other than stock.

Two examples of a tax straddle include:

1. Stock offset by a convertible debenture of the same corporation where the price movements of the two are related; and

2. Short position in a stock index regulated futures contract (RFC), or long put option on the RFC or an index, offset by stock in an investment company the performance of whose principal holdings mimics the index, or ownership of a portfolio of stocks whose performance mimics the performance of the stocks in the index.

The straddle sections coordinate with IRC Section 246 which sets forth the rules for determining the period for which a corporation's holding period of stock is tolled (for purposes of determining its eligibility for a dividend received deduction. Under Section 246(c)(4)(C), the offsetting position can include stock, whereas under Section 1092(d)(3)(B), the offsetting position must consist of property other than stock. Thus, only Prop. Regs. Section 1.2465(b), defining substantially similar or related property, applies for purposes of Section 1092(d)(3)(B).

A detailed discussion of the dividend received deduction is beyond the scope of this book and will only be considered to develop the definitions of a straddle.

Substantially similar or related property is defined in Prop. Regs. Section 1.2465(b)(2). Property will be considered substantially similar or related property if *both* of the following conditions are true:

1. The fair market value of the stock and the other property primarily reflect the performance of:

   (a) A single firm or enterprise; or

   (b) A single economic factor, such as (but not limited to) interest rates, commodity prices, or foreign currency exchange rates; and

2. Changes in the value of the stock are reasonably expected to approximate changes in the value of the property (positive or negative). Prop. Regs. Section 1.2465(b)(2)(i).

What does this mean? The straddle rules are concerned with investors holding offsetting positions to substantially diminish their risk of loss. In many cases, it may not be clear whether positions held by an investor are offsetting. To be treated as offsetting, the respective values of the positions must vary inversely. That is, an increase in the value of one position will be matched by a decrease in value of the other in about the same proportion. Also, they must offset the same economic factors, i.e., interest rates, currency rates, commodity prices, etc. Two diversified positions are not treated as offsetting even though losses in one or more such positions may sometimes be offset by gains in others.

The respective values of positions will vary inversely when the positions are contracts in the same personal property, or where a commodity is held and an offsetting contract of the same commodity is also held. Let's look at some examples:

Example 6-1

Ownership of a quantity of an actively traded commodity and a contract to sell part or all of the same commodity would be offsetting positions, as would a contractual obligation to make delivery of such commodity and a long futures contract on such commodity.

Example 6–2

A short call position on gold futures options and ownership of Krugerrands, Canadian Maple Leaf or other coins traded as a store of value would be offsetting.

Example 6–3

Similarly, a long position in soybean futures and a short position in soybean oil futures would be offsetting.

Example 6–4

A short futures position in wheat would not be offsetting to a long position in corn.

Example 6–5

Holding a Treasury note maturing in 20 years and a short T-bill futures contract should not be a straddle. However, a Treasury bill and a short T-bill futures contract would be a straddle.

Example 6–6

Holding nonparticipating fixed-term preferred stock in a corporation that has consistently paid dividends on the preferred and which is financially strong and a short position in Treasury securities with a similar maturity would be considered a straddle. If the preferred were participating it would not, since the stock's performance will depend on a number of economic factors other than interest rates.

What should be stressed is that there must be a reasonable expectation that changes in value of the two positions will vary inversely. A mere corresponding decrease of one position and increase in another is not enough to create a straddle. As you can imagine, these rules are not always easy to apply.

The Revenue Reconciliation Act of 1993 added an additional anti-abuse rule Section 1258, which provides that a portion of the income derived from certain *conversion transactions* must be treated as ordinary income rather than as capital gain. A conversion transaction is described as a transaction where substantially all of the taxpayer's return is attributable to interest on the taxpayer's net investment in the transaction. Gain is treated as ordinary to the extent it does not exceed interest that would have accrued on the taxpayer's net investment at a rate equal to 120% of the applicable federal rate. As interest rates have increased, Section 1258 will sweep up more and more transactions in its web.

Examples of conversion transactions include:

1. Holding property and entering into a contract to sell the property at a price determined in accordance with the contract, where the property was acquired and the contract was entered into on a substantially contemporaneous basis;

2. Certain straddles defined in IRC Section 1092(c) and certain straddles involving stocks;

3. Other transactions marketed or sold as producing capital gains; and

4. Other transactions designated by the Secretary.

Why are we so concerned with straddles? One answer is the KILLER RULE of Reg. Sec. 1-1092(b)-2T(b)(2). The killer rule generally provides that if the straddle is not identified and an election is not made to mark-to-market both sides, any loss is deferred until the offsetting position is disposed of and any loss will be capital and gain ordinary. The killer rule only works one way. The killer rule only applies to straddles in which all of the positions are capital assets.

Additionally, where the investor hedges a debt instrument with a notional principal contract, he must be sure to identify the straddle position under Section 1256(e)(2)(C) to avoid the loss deferral rule of Section 1092(a). Failure is lethal because it often means that a taxpayer with an active hedging program will be unable to net hedging activities.

CHAPTER 7

STRUCTURED DEBT INSTRUMENTS

OBJECTIVE

After completing this chapter you will understand:

- The basic economic and financial aspects of structured debt instruments.
- The basic tax principals relating to these products.

INTRODUCTION

The discussion in this section assumes that transactions do not come within the purview of Section 1259, which was added by the 1997 Tax Relief Act. That section, which affects short sales and certain other transactions, requires taxpayers to recognize gain (but not loss) on entering into a constructive sale of any appreciated position in stock, partnership interests, or certain debt instruments. If Section 1259 applies, gain is recognized as if the position were sold or terminated at its fair market value on the date of the constructive sale. Section 1259 applies to any constructive sale after June 8, 1997. A "constructive sale" for purposes of Section 1259 includes:

- A short sale of the same or substantially identical property,
- An "offsetting" notional principal contract with respect to the same or substantially identical property,
- A futures or forward contract to deliver the same or substantially identical property, or
- Other transactions having the same effect as the above transactions.

In the late eighties, many government agencies and government sponsored financing agencies (related privately owned corporations with a government purpose) began to issue structured debt instruments to meet their funding requirements. In an effort to raise money, these agencies have attempted to customize the cash flows of structure notes to closely match the investors' objectives. Investors may wish to implement a current interest rate or currency view, hedge a specific risk, balance portfolio characteristics, or simply to minimize transaction costs. Structured debt instruments in many ways have replaced interest rate (and other) swap and option arrangements without incurring the operational and transactional expenses required to establish and manage swap agreements and related counterparty credit risk.

Because structured notes can combine a variety of hedges in one debt instrument, a greater degree of sophistication is required to understand their intricacies. In fact, much of the public hysteria in the newspapers surrounding the huge losses incurred by some investors has revolved around a lack of understanding of the risks associated with these new structured debt instruments.

Different structures behave differently when interest rates, yield curves, exchange rates and other market indices change. Structured securities often do not involve a risk to the investor's principal; however, many contain features that can accelerate final maturities and place interest flows, and in some cases principal, at risk. As the variations expand, it is crucial to know exactly how the instrument is affected by market changes.

Callable Securities

A call feature allows the issuer to redeem the security on a given date or dates prior to maturity. Usually, the investor is compensated for the call feature in the form of a higher yield. Economically, the investor has sold an option to the issuer in exchange for a premium (higher yield on the instrument) paid over time. The value of the call option at any time depends on current market rates relative to the interest rate on the callable securities, the performance of the assets funded with the proceeds of callable securities, and the time remaining to the call date.

Issuers typically exercise call options in periods of declining interest rates, thereby creating re-investment risk (having to find alternative investments with the same or higher yield) for the investor. If the investor anticipates that the security will be called and it is not, the investor faces an extension of her anticipated maturity date which may or may not be desirable.

Step Securities

A step security is a security that pays an initial fixed interest rate until the call date. If the security has not been called, the interest rate "steps-up" to a higher rate, usually fixed prior to the issuance of the security. A single security can have more than one step-up period. Step-up securities are typically structured so that they are callable on an interest payment date.

Step securities can also call for a step-down in interest rates. These securities usually have a higher initial interest rate but greater uncertainty about maturity.

Indexed Amortization Notes

Indexed amortization notes, also known as indexed principal redemption bonds, principal amortization notes or indexed sinking fund debentures, pay a fixed rate of interest and repay principal according to an amortization schedule which is typically linked to the level of a designated interest rate such as the London Interbank Offer Rate (LIBOR). The amortization of principal payments usually begins after a certain period called the "lock-out" period. During the lock-out period, interest is paid on the initial principal amount and no amortization of principal occurs. After the lock-out period, investors receive repayments of principal, at an amortization rate tied to a designated index, and interest on the principal outstanding. At the stated maturity date, any outstanding principal is retired regardless of the level of the index.

Floating Rate Securities

Rather than pay a fixed rate of interest and later calling the debt instrument or changing the rate, floating rate instruments (floaters) offer interest rates which are tied to some interest rate index. Floaters were introduced during the seventies, a period of extreme interest rate volatility. Floaters offer enhanced yields compared to a strategy of continually rolling over short-term instruments and paying the related transaction costs. But the real advantage of floaters is that they allow the investor to match asset and liability cash flows.

The indices used to set the interest rate include the following: constant maturity treasury index (CMT); cost of funds index (published by the 11th District Federal Home Loan Bank), Federal Reserve commercial paper composite, Fed funds rate, LIBOR, prime rate and various treasury bill rates. Floaters are typically priced at a number of basis points (100th of one percent) over or under the designated index. This will depend on the index and the creditworthiness of the issuer. Once the spread (number of basis point difference from the index) is set, it is usually not changed. Therefore, changing interest rates affect the amount of interest paid but not the spread.

Floaters may be issued with any reset period (daily to any time prior to maturity), any payment period (usually monthly to maturity) and any maturity. Longer maturities usually carry a slight yield premium to cover the possibility of changes in the issuer's credit quality. Valuation is usually based on the volatility of the base index, the time to maturity, market interest rates and the credit quality or financial status of the issuer. The more dynamic the valuation factors, the more volatile the security is likely to be.

Callable Floaters

Callable floaters combine the floating rate instruments described above with a call feature. The call feature allows the issuer to redeem the securities before maturity. Unlike fixed rate instruments, issuers of floaters will exercise call provisions when interest rates are rising and refrain from exercising when interest rates are falling. Issuers may also include put options in a floater to accommodate investors who are compelled to invest in maturities of limited duration. A put option gives the investor the option of selling the debt instrument back to the issuer.

Inverse Floaters

Inverse floaters have interest rates which vary inversely to the general direction of interest rates. Inverse floaters are typically stated as a fixed rate of interest minus a specific index. As interest rates rise, the value of an inverse floater falls. Therefore, they perform well in declining interest rate environments but can experience disastrous results when interest rates rise.

Leveraged Floaters/Leveraged Inverse Floaters

These instruments have interest rates that reset a multiple of a given index plus a fixed rate (leveraged floaters) or at a fixed rate minus some multiple of the index (leveraged inverse floaters). Investors get a higher return if rates move in the anticipated direction, but also stand to lose more if their assumptions about the future course of interest rates are incorrect. The multiple creates additional upside potential and downside risk. Leveraged inverse floaters have been the recent culprit of the huge losses incurred by many mutual funds, corporations and even municipalities. This is not to say that they do not serve a purpose, but leverage does bring additional elements of risk.

Deleveraged Floaters/Deleveraged Inverse Floaters

Deleveraged floaters have interest rates that equal a fractional percentage of an index plus a spread. In a declining rate environment, the rate of interest declines only a percentage of the overall market decline giving the investor a better return than the ordinary floating rate instrument. In a rising rate environment, however, the performance of these securities will lag as the rate of interest only increases by a percentage of the absolute change in rates. A deleveraged inverse floater pays interest based on a fixed rate minus a fractional percentage of the index.

Step-Up Floaters/Step-Up Inverse Floaters

These debt securities have features that allow for changes in the formula for calculating the floating rate. A step-up floater will usually call for an increase in the spread to the index if the security is not called after a certain period. In a step-up inverse floater the fixed rate from which the index is subtracted increases.

Lower-Of and Higher-Of Floaters

These debt instruments pay an interest rate stated as the lower or higher of two different formulas. Investors structuring their portfolio to reflex a complex view of future interest rate movements, will usually invest in these types of instruments.

Range Securities

These debt instruments vary their interest rates within a range. Depending on the number of days, the designated index falls within or without an established range of interest rates. Should rates move beyond the range on either end, the investor faces the risk of a reduced or zero interest payment for the applicable interest period.

Multiple Index Floaters

These instruments have interest rates based on the difference between two interest rates indexes. These instruments allow investors to hedge risks on assets tied to each of the two interest rates.

Strike Securities

These debt instruments combine a fixed rate instrument with an inverse floater. These instruments pay a fixed rate of interest as long as the designated index rate remains below an established level. If the interest rate rises above the established level, then the interest rate changes to an inverse floater which subsequently decreases with increases in the index (and vice versa).

Yield Curve Securities

A yield curve is the charting of yields on a particular type of security over a spectrum of maturities ranging from three months to 30 years. These yield curve securities allow investors to implement a given yield curve view. If they expect the curve to flatten, they can purchase a structured security with a floating rate yield tied to a short-term index rate (e.g., three-month LIBOR) plus a spread minus, a long-term index rate (e.g., the ten-year CMT index). The interest paid on this security will increase as the short-term rate increases relative to the long-term rate. On the other hand, if the investor thinks the yield curve is going to steepen, the purchase of a floater indexed off a long-term rate minus a short-term rate could enhance the investor's yield.

TAXATION OF VARIABLE RATE DEBT INSTRUMENTS

Variable rate debt instruments are essentially debt instruments that bear a floating rate of interest. To qualify as a variable rate debt instrument, the instrument must require repayment of most of the principal and must provide stated interest at a qualified variable rate.[1] The issue price of the instrument must not be more than 115% of the sum of the total noncontingent payments.[2]

Stated interest must be payable at least annually or compounded at current values of:

1. One or more qualified floating rates;

2. A single fixed rate and one or more qualified floating rates;

3. A single objective rate; or

4. A single fixed rate and a single objective rate, that is, a qualified inverse floater.[3]

A floating rate is a qualified floating rate if variations in the rate can be reasonably expected to measure contemporaneous variations in the cost of newly borrowed funds in the currency in which the debt is denominated.[4] Typical qualified interest rates would include prime, Fed funds rate, LIBOR, yields on Treasuries and current yields on debt securities of a single issuer or a group of issuers. Required is a reasonable correlation between the rate and current borrowing costs; therefore, rates quoted in terms of basis point additions or subtractions will qualify. Rates stated as multiples of floating rates may not qualify if the correlation is lost.[5]

If a variable rate of interest is subject to a cap, collar, or floor which as of the issue date could be reasonably expected to change the yield of the instrument from the yield that would be expected absent the restriction (cap, collar, or floor), then it is not a qualified variable rate of interest.[6] If the variable rate can be reasonably expected to inversely reflect the contemporaneous variations in the cost of newly borrowed funds, the variable rate will be considered a qualified variable rate of interest.[7] However, significant front- or back-loading of the interest is not allowed.[8]

For purposes of calculating OID, reset bonds are treated as maturing on the date immediately preceding the reset and then being reissued as of the first date that the reset rate is in effect. A reset bond is a variable rate debt instrument.

ANALYSIS

Let's revisit the example we began this book with. As you remember, to demonstrate the analysis of a derivative financial product we considered the following complex derivative offered by the credit facility of a major international auto manufacturer (T). In the beginning of 1994, T issued an index or structured note. The interest payment was based on the following formula:

Principal * [16.5% − (2 * 3yr DKR Swap)], Min 0.

When we analyzed the instrument we uncovered that the interest coupon was based on a rate of 16.5% less two times the three year Danish kroner swap rate, but in no event could the investor be required to refund principal.

Given that the principal is guaranteed the instrument would be classified as debt. The guarantee is in the form of a Cap (described above as Min 0). Remember, a Cap is an interest rate agreement whereby one of the counterparties agrees to limit the floating rate of interest to a set rate. The Cap described above will prevent the interest payment from going below zero. For tax purposes, this use of a Cap (although reasonably expected to change the yield) would not cause the interest to be other than a qualified variable rate of interest.[9]

Since the rate of interest will decrease as interest rates increase, this derivative debt instrument contains an inverse floater. As described above, an inverse floater has an interest rate which varies inversely to the general direction of interest rates. The above inverse floater is stated as a fixed rate of interest minus 2 times the 3 year Danish kroner swap rate. As the interest rate rises, the value of the inverse floater falls. Therefore, the purpose of the inverse floater is to protect T against declining interest rates. Essentially, an inverse floater can be viewed as being long a fixed rate future and short a floating rate future. Usually, an inverse floating rate is based on an interest rate index. The 3 year Danish kroner swap rate will have to be determined by dealer quotes.

For tax purposes, the 3 year Danish kroner swap rate is not a qualified floating rate. Variations in the rate 3 year Danish kroner swap rate cannot be reasonably expected to measure contemporaneous variations in the cost of newly borrowed funds in the currency in which the debt is denominated. Since the debt instrument is denominated in U.S. dollars, it is anticipated that the 3 year Danish kroner swap rate will not measure variations in the U.S. interest rate. Therefore, the interest rate is not a qualified floating rate.

One point of interest: the rate chosen by T is a three year rate. Therefore, the instrument will have a constant maturity with regard to the inverse interest rate chosen. Typically, structured notes use a floating maturity, i.e., something tied to short-term treasury obligations. To continue, since the rate decreases at twice the rate of the three year Danish kroner, the investor has purchased a leveraged instrument. Lastly, a U.S. investor will have to bear the currency risk of the Danish kroner.

What risks was T trying to hedge? First, T has probably entered into a three-year currency swap (Danish kroner) combined with a short Cap. The counterparty will receive a fixed rate of interest and T will receive a floating rate of interest. The inverse floater (long fixed rate short floating rate interest rate future) will offset T's Danish interest rate risk. The leveraged Danish currency forward will offset T's currency risk, and the long Cap will limit T's interest rate exposure and ensure that the principal amount is not affected by changes in the interest rate. Therefore, the note will not have negative amortization.

Combining all the risks in one instrument makes it easier for T to control these risks. It also makes it a nightmare for investors. At this point, you were probably able to identify all the financial instruments imbedded within the instrument and even complex instruments like this one can be broken down into its component parts and analyzed.

SUMMARY

As you can see from the list of debt securities above, the combinations that an investor or issuer can create are endless. They are only limited by the creativity of parties. However, as you can also imagine the complexities regarding valuation of these instruments and how these instruments can be hedged can lead to nightmares when interest rates move in a direction the investor did not anticipate.

ENDNOTES

[1] Reg. Sec. 1.1275-5(a).

[2] Reg. Sec. 1.1275-5(a)(2).

[3] Reg. Sec. 1.1275-5(a)(3).

[4] Reg. Sec. 1.1275-5(b)(1).

[5] Reg. Sec. 1.1275-5(b)(2).

[6] Reg. Sec. 1.1275-5(b)(3).

[7] Reg. Sec. 1.1275-5(c)(3).

[8] Id.

[9] Reg. Sec. 1.1275-5(b)(3).

CHAPTER 8

REAL ESTATE MORTGAGE INVESTMENT CONDUITS (REMICS)

OBJECTIVE

After completing this chapter you will understand:

- The basic economic and financial aspects of REMICs.
- The basic tax principals relating to REMICs.

INTRODUCTION

Real Estate Mortgage Investment Conduits (REMICs) can contain complex distribution rules. Therefore, it is important to understand the fundamental REMIC structure (i.e., cash flow and sequential payment structure). Many REMICs have been designed to increase the predictability of cash flows associated with the prepayment possibility. Some REMICs have been specifically designed as a tool to serve an investor's liability and asset management strategy. Due to the flexibility of REMICs, investors should be extremely cautious. Certain portions of a REMIC can be highly sensitive to interest rates and unanticipated fluctuations can have material negative effects on yield and even failure by investors to recoup their principal investments.

DEFINITION

The Tax Reform Act of 1986 created the REMIC. The REMIC is a multiple-class mortgage cash flow security backed by mortgage-backed security certificates. A mortgage backed security (MBS) can be generally described as a security which is supported almost exclusively by payments from an underlying pool of mortgages. Economically they can be distinguished from conventional debt in that if the underlying mortgages that fund the MBS are prepaid, they will be subject to mandatory principal calls. Because of this prepayment feature, a whole host of economic, financial and tax issues arise.

Given the nature of an MBS, if material incremental taxes could not be avoided by the issuer, the issue would not be economically viable MBS. The REMIC legislation introduced by the Tax Reform Act of 1986 offered an entity the assurance that, if the income and distribution rules are followed, no tax will be paid by the REMIC.

REMICs can contain complex distribution rules: therefore, it is important to understand the fundamental REMIC structure (i.e., cash flow and sequential payment structure). Many REMICs have been designed to increase the predictability of cash flows associated with the prepayment possibility. Some REMICs have been specifically designed as a tool to serve an investor's liability and asset management strategy. Due to the flexibility of REMICs, investors should be extremely cautious. Certain portions of a REMIC can be highly sensitive to interest rates and unanticipated fluctuations can have material negative effects on yield and even failure by investors to recoup their principal investments.

DESCRIPTION OF THE BASIC REMIC TRANCHES

Sequential Pay Tranches

Sequential pay tranches are the most basic classes. A tranche can best be described as specific group of interest and/or principal cash flows which are allocated to a class. Sequential pay tranches are retired sequentially. Typically, tranches are labeled A through Z. The lower lettered tranches have the shortest maturities. Each sequential pay tranche receives allocated interest payments each month; however, all other cash flows, including prepayments, are directed to the A tranche until it is retired. In sequence, each tranche begins to receive principal payments and is retired.

Planned Amortization Class (PAC) Tranches

In addition to the standard tranches a REMIC often has PAC tranches. A PAC is similar to a sinking fund bond and offers the investor the greatest degree of cash flow certainty. The PAC investor is scheduled to receive payments over a predetermined period of time under a range of prepayment possibilities. The cash flows are arranged to give PAC investors first right over other class holders. The PAC investor is also protected from faster than expected prepayments. These prepayments support other tranches first and insulate the PAC investor from increasing prepayments. In essence, the investor has a sort of call protection.

Usually, there is a defined minimum and maximum prepayment speed under which the PAC scheduled prepayment will remain unchanged. The average life, duration and cash flow yield of a PAC tranche varies little if prepayments remain fairly constant within the protected range. However, when prepayments vary greatly (even though prepayment speeds are within the protected range) the investor could experience a month or two without payments. The current effective range of PAC tranches can differ from the protected range at issuance. This is due primarily to changes in the paydown of the underlying MBS.

The non-PAC tranches (support or companion tranches) bear the real risk of varying prepayments. These tranches absorb excess cash flows and make up shortfalls. Therefore, the average life of a support tranche will be extremely variable, varying directly with the underlying cash flows from the MBS.

Targeted Amortization Classes (TAC)

TACs are similar to PACs. A TAC is designed to pay a specified or "targeted" amount of principal to a class holder each month. The TAC structure typically provides protection against increasing prepayments and early retirement of the investment. If prepayments increase, excess cash flow will be paid to the support tranches, not toward retirement of the TAC tranche. If prepayments are slow, the average life of the TAC tranche will be extended. TACs provide higher yields than PACs for accepting greater prepayment uncertainty.

Companion (Support) Tranches

Companion (support) tranches receive any excess cash flows and absorb any cash shortfalls generated by the underlying MBS. These tranches experience greater fluctuations in duration cash flows. The duration of support tranches will be extended in periods of rising interest rates and be shorter when interest rates are falling. Yields are especially sensitive to interest rates, especially if the investor purchases the tranche for a discount or premium. Tranches supporting PACs are more sensitive than those supporting TACs, because PACs are protected within a range. The companion classes supporting both PACs and TACs will receive their principal repayment cash flows earlier than expected if prepayments increase. If prepayments slow, the repayment of principal for TAC and companion tranches will also slow. Companion tranches are subject to greater duration risk in rising interest rate environments. Therefore, companion tranches have more price sensitivity in rising rate environments and become less price sensitive in a falling rate environment, when the duration risk is lower.

Z or Accrual Tranches

The final regular class of a REMIC is called the Z or accrual tranche. A Z tranche can also include other classes. This class receives no interest payments until certain other classes are paid down. Interest accrues and the balance of the Z tranche grows at the coupon rate until the applicable classes are retired. When the applicable classes are retired, the Z tranche converts to an ordinary interest paying mortgage security that pays down principal monthly until fully amortized. In some REMICs, the Z tranche functions much like a zero coupon or stripped Treasury bond and does not receive any interest. Instead, interest accruals continue until the REMIC pays off. In that case, all prepayments are considered redemptions of principal.

The function of the Z tranche is to accelerate the paydown of other tranches by providing other tranches with additional cash flow. The Z tranche takes the place of another intermediate class but receives no cash flow. Therefore, the cash flow can be used to support other tranches.

Interest Only/Principal Only (IO/PO)

REMIC structures often include two classes which are created by stripping apart the interest and principal components from the standard MBS. Each class is allocated either the monthly interest and principal payments from the underlying collateral. The IO and PO tranches are very sensitive to interest rates and principal prepayments. An investor who pays a premium to receive a certain yield on an IO or PO is extremely vulnerable to interest rate changes as prepayments could result in early retirement of the class, in which case the investor has paid a premium and may not have received interest equal to the premium.

TAXATION OF REMIC INTERESTS

For Federal income tax purposes, REMICs are divided into regular and residual interests. REMIC regular interest classes are considered debt instruments. Therefore, the OID, market discount and premium amortization rules, previously discussed, will apply. Accordingly, REMIC income is calculated using the accrual method of accounting.

Although REMIC taxable income may or may not approximate the REMIC's cash flow, the components of REMIC taxable income are affected by principal prepayments on the underlying mortgages. REMIC taxable income is also affected by the class's yield to maturity and the REMIC's principal distribution rules.

Before continuing, readers should re-acquaint themselves with the tax concepts discussed in Chapters 1, 5 and 6. Specifically: OID, stated redemption price at maturity, adjusted issue price, market discount and premium, and bond premium. The following paragraphs will review the tax concepts of REMICs by considering different examples.

Assumptions:

>   The OID regulations provide an election to treat all payments on the regular interest of a REMIC as OID. This would include coupon interest, OID, market discount, acquisition premium and bond premium. The examples below assume that this election has not been made.

>   Assume for purposes of the following examples that Bond A has a stated redemption price at maturity of $10,000. The principal is paid in full in year 10, and annual interest payments of $1,000 per year are qualified interest.

OID

OID is the difference between the debt instrument's stated redemption price at maturity and its issue price. Stated redemption price at maturity is generally all amounts projected to be received on the class except qualified interest. Qualified interest is generally the stated coupon rate of interest. Qualified interest can be based on a fixed or variable rate. A holder of a debt instrument issued with qualified interest paid annually, reports taxable interest income equal to the amount of interest which is includible based on the taxpayer's method of accounting.

> ### Example 8–1
>
> Assume DBL purchases Bond A at original issue price of $9,250. Because the principal is paid in full in year 10, and qualified interest is paid annually, Bond A will have $750 of OID (stated redemption price at maturity $10,000 less issue price $9,250).

Adjusted Issue Price

Adjusted issue price is the bond's issue price less any payments made on the instrument other than qualified interest, plus OID included in taxable income.

> ### Example 8–2
>
> If we assume that Bond A (in Example 1) has $50 of OID which is included in income, the adjusted issue price would be $9,300 ($9,250 issue price plus $50 OID included in taxable income).

Market Discount

If an investor acquires an OID bond in the secondary market (not from the original issuer) at a price lower than the bond's adjusted issue price the bond will have market discount. Market discount is the difference between the investor's cost basis and the bond's adjusted issue price.

> ### Example 8–3
>
> Assume DBL sells Bond A (above) for $9,000 to LBD. LBD will have purchased a bond with $300 of market discount ($9,300 adjusted issue price less LBD's cost of $9,000).

Acquisition Premium

If an investor acquires an OID bond in the secondary market (not from the original issuer) at a price greater than the bond's adjusted issue price but below the bond's stated redemption price at maturity, the bond will have acquisition premium. Acquisition premium is the difference between the investor's cost basis and the bond's adjusted issue price.

> ### Example 8–4
>
> Assume DBL sells Bond A (above) for $9,500 to LBD. LBD will have purchased a bond with $200 of acquisition premium (LBD's cost of $9,500 less $9,300, the bond's adjusted issue price).

Interest Only/Principal Only Bonds

Example 8-5

Assume the interest payments on bond A are sold to DBL for $5,000 and the principal payments are sold to LBD for $4,000. The interest portion is an IO strip and the principal portion is a PO strip. The IO provides for annual interest payments of $1,000 for ten years. An IO/PO has no qualified interest; therefore, any amounts payable will be considered part of the stated redemption price at maturity. The stated redemption price of the IO is the total payments to be received, $10,000. The IO will have OID of $5,000 (stated redemption price at maturity $10,000 less issue price $5,000). The PO would have OID of $6,000 (stated redemption price at maturity $10,000 less issue price $4,000).

Accrual Bonds

Example 8-6

Assume investor DBL acquires Bond A for $9,250. Assume further, the bond has a stated redemption price at maturity of $20,000, the sum of all payments to be received on the bond. The bond has $10,750 of OID (stated redemption price at maturity $20,000 less issue price $9,250).